The Case for India
&
The Basis of Morality

Annie Besant

CONTENTS

THE CASE FOR INDIA

THE BASIS OF MORALITY

PRESIDENTIAL ADDRESS

Fellow-delegates and friends,

Everyone who has preceded me in this Chair has rendered his thanks in fitting terms for the gift which is truly said to be the highest that India has it in her power to bestow. It is the sign of her fullest love, trust, and approval, and the one whom she seats in that chair is, for his year of service, her chosen leader. But if my predecessors found fitting words for their gratitude, in what words can I voice mine, whose debt to you is so overwhelmingly greater than theirs? For the first time in Congress history, you have chosen as your President one who, when your choice was made, was under the heavy ban of Government displeasure, and who lay interned as a person dangerous to public safety. While I was humiliated, you crowned me with honour; while I was slandered, you believed in my integrity and good faith; while I was crushed under the heel of bureaucratic power, you acclaimed me as your leader; while I was silenced and unable to defend myself, you defended me, and won for me release. I was proud to serve in lowliest fashion, but you lifted me up and placed me before the world as your chosen representative. I have no words with which to thank you, no eloquence with which to repay my debt. My deeds must speak for me, for words are too poor. I turn your gift into service to the Motherland; I consecrate my life anew to her in worship by action. All that I have and am, I lay on the Altar of the Mother, and together we shall cry, more by service than by words: VANDE MATARAM

There is, perhaps, one value in your election of me in this crisis of India's destiny, seeing that I have not the privilege to be Indian-born, but come from that little island in the northern seas which has been, in the West, the builder-up of free institutions. The Aryan emigrants, who spread over the lands of Europe, carried with them the seeds of liberty sown in their blood in their Asian cradle-land. Western historians trace the self-rule of the Saxon villages to their earlier prototypes in the East, and see the growth of English liberty as up-springing from the Aryan root of the free and self-contained village communities.

Its growth was crippled by Norman feudalism there, as its millennia-nourished security here was smothered by the East India Company. But in England it burst its shackles and nurtured a liberty-loving people and a free Commons' House. Here, it similarly bourgeoned out into the Congress activities, and more recently into those of the Muslim League, now together blossoming into Home Rule for India. The England of Milton, Cromwell, Sydney, Burke, Paine, Shelley, Wilberforce, Gladstone; the England that sheltered Mazzini, Kossuth, Kropotkin, Stepniak, and that welcomed Garibaldi; the England that is the enemy of tyranny, the foe of autocracy, the lover of freedom, that is the England I would fain here represent to you to-day. To-day, when India stands erect, no suppliant people, but a Nation, self-conscious, self-respecting, determined to be free; when she stretches out her hand to Britain and offers friendship not subservience; co-operation not obedience; to-day let me: western-born but in spirit eastern, cradled in England but Indian by choice and adoption: let me stand as the symbol of union between Great Britain and India: a union of hearts and free choice, not of compulsion: and therefore of a tie which cannot be broken, a tie of love and of mutual helpfulness, beneficial to both Nations and blessed by God.

GONE TO THE PEACE

India's great leader, Dadabhai Naoroji, has left his mortal body and is now one of the company of the Immortals, who watch over and aid India's progress. He is with V.C. Bonnerjee, and Ranade, and A.O. Hume, and Henry Cotton, and Pherozeshah Mehta, and Gopal Krishna Gokhale: the great men who, in Swinburne's noble verse, are the stars which lead us to Liberty's altar:

> These, O men, shall ye honour,
> Liberty only and these.
> For thy sake and for all men's and mine,
> Brother, the crowns of them shine,
> Lighting the way to her shrine,
> That our eyes may be fastened upon her,
> That our hands may encompass her knees.

Not for me to praise him in feeble words of reverence or of homage. His deeds praise him, and his service to his country is his abiding glory. Our gratitude will be best paid by following in his footsteps, alike in his splendid courage and his unfaltering devotion, so that we may win the Home Rule which he longed to see while with us, and shall see, ere long, from the other world of Life, in which he dwells today.

THE CASE FOR INDIA

CHAPTER I

PRE-WAR MILITARY EXPENDITURE

The Great War, into the whirlpool of which Nation after Nation has been drawn, has entered on its fourth year. The rigid censorship which has been established makes it impossible for any outside the circle of Governments to forecast its duration, but to me, speaking for a moment not as a politician but as a student of spiritual laws, to me its end is sure. For the true object of this War is to prove the evil of, and to destroy, autocracy and the enslavement of one Nation by another, and to place on sure foundations the God-given Right to Self-Rule and Self-Development of every Nation, and the similar right of the Individual, of the smaller Self, so far as is consistent with the welfare of the larger Self of the Nation. The forces which make for the prolongation of autocracy—the rule of one—and the even deadlier bureaucracy—the rule of a close body welded into an iron system—these have been gathered together in the Central Powers of Europe—as of old in Ravana—in order that they may be destroyed; for the New Age cannot be opened until the Old passes away. The new civilisation of Righteousness and Justice, and

2

therefore of Brotherhood, of ordered Liberty, of Peace, of Happiness, cannot be built up until the elements are removed which have brought the old civilisation crashing about our ears. Therefore is it necessary that the War shall be fought out to its appointed end, and that no premature peace shall leave its object unattained. Autocracy and bureaucracy must perish utterly, in East and West, and, in order that their germs may not re-sprout in the future, they must be discredited in the minds of men. They must be proved to be less efficient than the Governments of Free Peoples, even in their favourite work of War, and their iron machinery—which at first brings outer prosperity and success—must be shown to be less lasting and effective than the living and flexible organisations of democratic Peoples. They must be proved failures before the world, so that the glamour of superficial successes may be destroyed for ever. They have had their day and their place in evolution, and have done their educative work. Now they are out-of-date, unfit for survival, and must vanish away.

When Great Britain sprang to arms, it was in defence of the freedom of a small nation, guaranteed by treaties, and the great principles she proclaimed electrified India and the Dominions. They all sprang to her side without question, without delay; they heard the voice of old England, the soldier of Liberty, and it thrilled their hearts. All were unprepared, save the small territorial army of Great Britain, due to the genius and foresight of Lord Haldane, and the readily mobilised army of India, hurled into the fray by the swift decision of Lord Hardinge. The little army of Britain fought for time; fought to stop the road to Paris, the heart of France; fought, falling back step by step, and gained the time it fought for, till India's sons stood on the soil of France, were flung to the front, rushed past the exhausted regiments who cheered them with failing breath, charged the advancing hosts, stopped the retreat, and joined the British army in forming that unbreakable line which wrestled to the death through two fearful winters—often, these soldiers of the tropics, waist-deep in freezing mud—and knew no surrender.

India, with her clear vision, saw in Great Britain the champion of Freedom, in Germany the champion of Despotism. And she saw rightly. Rightly she stood by Great Britain, despite her own lack of freedom and the coercive legislation which outrivalled German despotism, knowing these to be temporary, because un-English, and therefore doomed to destruction; she spurned the lure of German gold and rejected German appeals to revolt. She offered men and money; her educated classes, her Vakils, offered themselves as Volunteers, pleaded to be accepted. Then the never-sleeping distrust of Anglo-India rejected the offer, pressed for money, rejected men. And, slowly, educated India sank back, depressed and disheartened, and a splendid opportunity for knitting together the two Nations was lost.

Early in the War I ventured to say that the War could not end until England recognised that autocracy and bureaucracy must perish in India as well as in Europe. The good Bishop of Calcutta, with a courage worthy of his free race, lately declared that it would be hypocritical to pray for victory over autocracy in Europe and to maintain it in India. Now it has been clearly and definitely declared that Self-Government is to be the objective of Great Britain in India, and that a substantial measure of it is to be given at once; when this promise is made good by the granting of the Reforms outlined last year in Lucknow, then the end of the War will be in sight. For the War cannot end till the death-knell of autocracy is sounded.

Causes, with which I will deal presently and for which India was not responsible, have somewhat obscured the first eager

4

expressions of India's sympathy, and have forced her thoughts largely towards her own position in the Empire. But that does not detract from the immense aid she has given, and is still giving. It must not be forgotten that long before the present War she had submitted—at first, while she had no power of remonstrance, and later, after 1885, despite the constant protests of Congress—to an ever-rising military expenditure, due partly to the amalgamation scheme of 1859, and partly to the cost of various wars beyond her frontiers, and to continual recurring frontier and trans-frontier expeditions, in which she had no real interest. They were sent out for supposed Imperial advantages, not for her own.

Between 1859 and 1904—45 years—Indian troops were engaged in thirty-seven wars and expeditions. There were ten wars: the two Chinese Wars of 1860 and 1900, the Bhutan War of 1864-65, the Abyssinian War of 1868, the Afghan War of 1878-79, and, after the massacre of the Kabul Mission, the second War of 1879-80, ending in an advance of the frontier, in the search for an ever receding "scientific frontier"; on this occasion the frontier was shifted, says Keene, "from the line of the Indus to the western slope of the Suleiman range and from Peshawar to Quetta"; the Egyptian War of 1882, in which the Indian troops markedly distinguished themselves; the third Burmese War of 1885 ending in the annexation of Upper Burma in 1886; the invasions of Tibet in 1890 and 1904. Of Expeditions, or minor Wars, there were 27; to Sitana in 1858 on a small scale and in 1863 on a larger (the "Sitana Campaign"); to Nepal and Sikkim in 1859; to Sikkim in 1864; a serious struggle on the North-west Frontier in 1868; expeditions against the Lushais in 1871-72, the Daflas in 1874-75, the Nagas in 1875, the Afridis in 1877, the Rampa Hill tribes in 1879, the Waziris and Nagas in 1881, the Akhas in 1884, and in the same year an

5

expedition to the Zhob Valley, and a second thither in 1890. In 1888 and 1889 there was another expedition against Sikkim, against the Akozais (the Black Mountain Expedition) and against the Hill Tribes of the North-east, and in 1890 another Black Mountain Expedition, with a third in 1892. In 1890 came the expedition to Manipur, and in 1891 there was another expedition against the Lushais, and one into the Miranzal Valley. The Chitral Expedition occupied 1894-95, and the serious Tirah Campaign, in which 40,000 men were engaged, came in 1897 and 1898. The long list—which I have closed with 1904—ends with the expeditions against the Mahsuds in 1901, against the Kabalis in 1902, and the invasion of Tibet, before noted. All these events explain the rise in military expenditure, and we must add to them the sending of Indian troops to Malta and Cyprus in 1878—a somewhat theatrical demonstration—and the expenditure of some £2,000,000 to face what was described as "the Russian Menace" in 1884. Most of these were due to Imperial, not to Indian, policy, and many of the burdens imposed were protested against by the Government of India, while others were encouraged by ambitious Viceroys. I do not think that even this long list is complete.

Ever since the Government of India was taken over by the Crown, India has been regarded as an Imperial military asset and training ground, a position from which the jealousy of the East India Company had largely protected her, by insisting that the army it supported should be used for the defence and in the interests of India alone. Her value to the Empire for military purposes would not so seriously have injured at once her pride and her finances if the natural tendencies of her martial races had been permitted their previous scope; but the disarming of the people, 20 years after the assumption of the Government by the Crown, emasculated the

6

Nation, and the elimination of races supposed to be unwarlike, or in some cases too warlike to be trusted, threw recruitment more and more to the north, and lowered the physique of the Bengalis and Madrasis, on whom the Company had largely depended.

The superiority of the Punjab, on which Sir Michael O'Dwyer so vehemently insisted the other day, is an artificial superiority, created by the British system and policy; and the poor recruitment elsewhere, on which he laid offensive insistence, is due to the same system and policy, which largely eliminated Bengalis, Madrasis and Mahrattas from the army. In Bengal, however, the martial type has been revived, chiefly in consequence of what the Bengalis felt to be the intolerable insult of the high-handed Partition of Bengal by Lord Curzon.

On this Gopal Krishna Gokhale said:

> Bengal's heroic stand against the oppression of a harsh and uncontrolled bureaucracy has astonished and gratified all India.... All India owes a deep debt of gratitude to Bengal.

The spirit evoked showed itself in the youth of Bengal by a practical revolt, led by the elders, while it was confined to Swadeshi and Boycott, and rushing on, when it broke away from their authority, into conspiracy, assassination and dacoity: as had happened in similar revolts with Young Italy, in the days of Mazzini, and with Young Russia in the days of Stepniak and Kropotkin. The results of their despair, necessarily met by the halter and penal servitude, had to be faced by Lord Hardinge and Lord Carmichael during the present War. Other results, happy instead of disastrous in their nature, was the development of grit and endurance of a high character, shown in the courage of the Bengal lads in the serious floods that have laid parts of the Province deep under water, and in their compassion and self-sacrifice in the relief of famine. Their services in the present War—the Ambulance Corps and the replacement of its materiel when the ship carrying it sank, with the splendid services rendered by it in Mesopotamia; the recruiting of a Bengali regiment for active service, 900 strong, with another 900 reserves to replace wastage, and recruiting still going on—these are instances of the divine alchemy which brings the soul of good out of evil action, and consecrates to service the qualities evoked by rebellion.

In England, also, a similar result has been seen in a convict, released to go to the front, winning the Victoria Cross. It would be an act of statesmanship, as well as of divinest compassion, to offer to every prisoner and interned captive, held for political crime or on political suspicion, the opportunity of serving the Empire at the front. They might, if thought necessary, form a separate battalion or a separate regiment, under stricter supervision, and yet be given a chance of redeeming their reputation, for they are mostly very young.

The financial burden incurred in consequence of the above conflicts, and of other causes, now to be mentioned, would not have been so much resented, if it had been imposed by India on herself, and if her own sons had profited by her being used as a training ground for the Empire. But in this case, as in so many others, she has shared Imperial burdens, while not sharing Imperial freedom and power. Apart from this, the change which made the Army so ruinous a burden on the resources of the country was the system of "British reliefs," the using of India as a training ground for British regiments, and the transfer of the men thus trained, to be replaced by new ones under the short service system, the cost of the frequent transfers and their connected expenses being charged on the Indian revenues, while the whole advantage was reaped by Great Britain. On the short service system the Simla Army Commission declared:

The short service system recently introduced into the British Army has increased the cost and has materially reduced the efficiency of the British troops in India. We cannot resist the feeling that, in the introduction of this system, the interest of the Indian tax-payer was entirely left out of consideration.

The remark was certainly justified, for the short service system gave India only five years of the recruits she paid heavily for and trained, all the rest of the benefit going to England. The latter was enabled, as the years went on, to enormously increase her Reserves, so that she has had 400,000 men trained in, and at the cost of, India.

In 1863 the Indian army consisted of 140,000 men, with 65,000 white officers. Great changes were made in 1885-1905, including the reorganisation under Lord Kitchener, who became Commander-in-Chief at the end of 1902. Even in this hasty review, I must not omit reference to the fact that Army Stores were drawn from Britain at enormous cost, while they should have been chiefly manufactured here, so that India might have profited by the expenditure. Lately under the necessities of War, factories have been turned to the production of munitions; but this should have been done long ago, so that India might have been enriched instead of exploited. The War has forced an investigation into her mineral resources that might have been made for her own sake, but Germany was allowed to monopolise the supply of minerals that India could have produced and worked up, and would have produced and worked up had she enjoyed Home Rule. India would have been richer, and the Empire safer, had she been a partner instead of a possession. But this side of the question will come under the matters directly affecting merchants, and we may venture to express a hope that the Government help extended to munition factories in time of War may be continued to industrial factories in time of Peace. The net result of the various causes above-mentioned was that the expense of the Indian army rose by leaps and bounds, until, before the War, India was expending,£21,000,000 as against the £28,000,000 expended by the United Kingdom, while the wealthy Dominions of Canada and Australia were spending only 1-1/2 and 1-1/4 millions respectively. (I am not forgetting that the United Kingdom was expending over £51,000,000 on her Navy, while India was free of that burden, save for a contribution of half a million.)

Since 1885, the Congress has constantly protested against the ever-increasing military expenditure, but the voice of the Congress was supposed to be the voice of sedition and of class ambition, instead of being, as it was the voice of educated Indians, the most truly patriotic and loyal class of the population. In 1885, in the First Congress, Mr. P. Rangiah Naidu pointed out that military expenditure had been £1,463,000 in 1857 and had risen to £16,975,750 in 1884. Mr. D.E. Wacha ascribed the growth to the amalgamation scheme of 1859, and remarked that the Company in 1856 had an army of 254,000 men at a cost of 11-1/2 millions, while in 1884 the Crown had an army of only 181,000 men at a cost of 17 millions. The rise was largely due to the increased cost of the European regiments, overland transport service, stores, pensions, furlough allowances, and the like, most of them imposed despite the resistance of the Government of India, which complained that the changes were "made entirely, it may be said, from Imperial considerations, in which Indian interests have not been consulted or advanced." India paid nearly,£700,000 a year, for instance, for "Home Depôts"—Home being England of course—in which lived some 20,000 to 22,000 British soldiers, on the plea that their regiments, not they, were serving in India. I cannot follow out the many increases cited by Mr. Wacha, but members can refer to his excellent speech.

Mr. Fawcett once remarked that when the East India Company was abolished

> the English people became directly responsible for the Government of India. It cannot, I think, be denied that this responsibility has been so imperfectly discharged that in many respects the new system of Government compares unfavourably with the old.... There was at that time an independent control of expenditure which now seems to be almost entirely wanting.

Shortly after the Crown assumed the rule of India, Mr. Disraeli asked the House of Commons to regard India as "a great and solemn trust committed to it by an all-wise and inscrutable Providence." Mr. George Yule, in the Fourth Congress, remarked on this: "The 650 odd members had thrown the trust back upon the hands of Providence, to be looked after as Providence itself thinks best." Perhaps it is time that India should remember that Providence helps those who help themselves.

Year after year the Congress continued to remonstrate against the cost of the army, until in 1902, after all the futile protests of the intervening years, it condemned an increase of pay to British soldiers in India which placed an additional burden on the Indian revenues of £786,000 a year, and pointed out that the British garrison was unnecessarily numerous, as was shown by the withdrawal of large bodies of British soldiers for service in South Africa and China. The very next year Congress protested that the increasing military expenditure was not to secure India against internal disorder or external attack, but in order to carry out an

Imperial policy; the Colonies contributed little or nothing to the Imperial Military Expenditure, while India bore the cost of about one-third of the whole British Army in addition to her own Indian troops. Surely these facts should be remembered when India's military services to the Empire are now being weighed.

In 1904 and 1905, the Congress declared that the then military expenditure was beyond India's power to bear, and in the latter year prayed that the additional ten millions sterling sanctioned for Lord Kitchener's reorganisation scheme might be devoted to education and the reduction of the burden on the raiyats. In 1908, the burdens imposed by the British War Office since 1859 were condemned, and in the next year it was pointed out that the military expenditure was nearly a third of the whole Indian revenue, and was starving Education and Sanitation.

Lord Kitchener's reorganisation scheme kept the Indian Army on a War footing, ready for immediate mobilisation, and on January 1, 1915, the regular army consisted of 247,000 men, of whom 75,000 were English; it was the money spent by India in maintaining this army for years in readiness for War which made it possible for her to go to the help of Great Britain at the critical early period to which I alluded. She spent over £20 millions on the military services in 1914-15. In 1915-16 she spent £21.8 millions. In 1916-17 her military budget had risen to £12 millions, and it will probably be exceeded, as was the budget of the preceding year by £1-2/3 million.

Lord Hardinge, the last Viceroy of India, who is ever held in loving memory here for his sympathetic attitude towards Indian aspirations, made a masterly exposition of India's War services in the House of Lords on the third of last July. He emphasised her pre-War services, showing that though 19-1/4 millions sterling was fixed as a maximum by the Nicholson Committee, that amount had been exceeded in 11 out of the last 13 budgets, while his own last budget had risen to 22 millions. During these 13 years the revenue had been only between 48 and 58 millions, once rising to 60 millions. Could any fact speak more eloquently of India's War services than this proportion of military expenditure compared with her revenue?

The Great War began on August 4th, and in that very month and in the early part of September, India sent an expeditionary force of three divisions—two infantry and one cavalry—and another cavalry division joined them in France in November. The first arrived, said Lord Hardinge, "in time to fill a gap that could not otherwise have been filled." He added pathetically: "There are very few survivors of those two splendid divisions of infantry." Truly, their homes are empty, but their sons shall enjoy in India the liberty for which their fathers died in France. Three more divisions were at once sent to guard the Indian frontier, while in September a mixed division was sent to East Africa, and in October and November two more divisions and a brigade of cavalry went to Egypt. A battalion of Indian infantry went to Mauritius, another to the Cameroons, and two to the Persian Gulf, while other Indian troops helped the Japanese in the capture of Tsingtau. 210,000 Indians were thus sent overseas. The whole of these troops were fully armed and equipped, and in addition, during the first few weeks of the War, India sent to England from her magazines "70 million rounds of small-arm ammunition, 60,000 rifles, and more than 550 guns of the latest pattern and type."

In addition to these, Lord Hardinge speaks of sending to England

enormous quantities of material, ... tents, boots, saddlery, clothing, etc., but every effort was made to meet the ever-increasing demands made by the War Office, and it may be stated without exaggeration that India was bled absolutely white during the first few weeks of the war.

It must not be forgotten, though Lord Hardinge has not reckoned it, that all wastage has been more than filled up, and 450,000 men represent this head; the increase in units has been 300,000, and including other military items India had placed in the field up to the end of 1916 over a million of men.

In addition to this a British force of 80,000 was sent from India, fully trained and equipped at Indian cost, India receiving in exchange, many months later, 34 Territorial battalions and 29 batteries, "unfit for immediate employment on the frontier or in Mesopotamia, until they had been entirely re-armed and equipped, and their training completed."

Between the autumn of 1914 and the close of 1915, the defence of our own frontiers was a serious matter, and Lord Hardinge says:

> The attitude of Afghanistan was for a long time doubtful, although I always had confidence in the personal loyalty of our ally the Amir; but I feared lest he might be overwhelmed by a wave of fanaticism, or by a successful Jehad of the tribes.... It suffices to mention that, although during the previous three years there had been no operations of any importance on the North-West frontier, there were, between November 29, 1914, and September 5, 1915, no less than seven serious attacks on the North-West frontier, all of which were effectively dealt with.

The military authorities had also to meet a German conspiracy early in 1915, 7,000 men arriving from Canada and the United States,

14

having planned to seize points of military vantage in the Panjab, and in December of the same year another German conspiracy in Bengal, necessitating military preparations on land, and also naval patrols in the Bay of Bengal.

Lord Hardinge has been much attacked by the Tory and Unionist Press in England and India, in England because of the Mesopotamia Report, in India because his love for India brought him hatred from Anglo-India. India has affirmed her confidence in him, and with India's verdict he may well rest satisfied.

I do not care to dwell on the Mesopotamia Commission and its condemnation of the bureaucratic system prevailing here. Lord Hardinge vindicated himself and India. The bureaucratic system remains undefended. I recall that bureaucratic inefficiency came out in even more startling fashion in connection with the Afghan War of 1878-79 and 1879-80. In February 1880, the war charges were reported as under £4 millions, and the accounts showed a surplus of £2 millions. On April 8th the Government of India reported: "Outgoing for War very alarming, far exceeding estimate," and on the 13th April "it was announced that the cash balances had fallen in three months from thirteen crores to less than nine, owing to 'excessive Military drain' ... On the following day (April 22) a despatch was sent out to the Viceroy, showing that there appeared a deficiency of not less than 5-1/4 crores. This vast error was evidently due to an underestimate of war liabilities, which had led to such mis-information being laid before Parliament, and to the sudden discovery of inability to 'meet the usual drawings.'"

It seemed that the Government knew only the amount audited, not the amount spent. Payments were entered as "advances," though they were not recoverable, and "the great negligence was evidently that of the heads of departmental accounts." If such a mishap should occur under Home Rule, a few years hence—which heaven forbid—I shudder to think of the comments of the Englishman and the Madras Mail on the shocking inefficiency of Indian officials.

In September last, our present Viceroy, H.E. Lord Chelmsford, defended India against later attacks by critics who try to minimise her sacrifices in order to lessen the gratitude felt by Great Britain towards her, lest that gratitude should give birth to justice, and justice should award freedom to India. Lord Chelmsford placed before his Council "in studiously considered outline, a summary of what India has done during the past two years." Omitting his references to what was done under Lord Hardinge, as stated above, I may quote from him:

> On the outbreak of war, of the 4,598 British officers on the Indian establishment, 530 who were at home on leave were detained by the War Office for service in Europe. 2,600 Combatant Officers have been withdrawn from India since the beginning of the War, excluding those who proceeded on service with their batteries or regiments. In order to make good these deficiencies and provide for war wastage the Indian Army Reserve of Officers was expanded from a total of 40, at which it stood on the 4th August, 1914, to one of 2,000.

> The establishment of Indian units has not only been kept up to strength, but has been considerably increased. There has been an augmentation of 20 per cent. in the cavalry and of 40 per cent. in the infantry, while the number of recruits enlisted since the beginning of the War is greater than the entire strength of the Indian Army as it existed on August 4, 1914.

Lord Chelmsford rightly pointed out:

> The Army in India has thus proved a great Imperial asset,
> and in weighing the value of India's contribution to the
> War it should be remembered that India's forces were no
> hasty improvisation, but were an army in being, fully
> equipped and supplied, which had previously cost India
> annually a large sum to maintain.

Lord Chelmsford has established what he calls a "Man-Power
Board," the duty of which is "to collect and co-ordinate all the facts
with regard to the supply of man-power in India." It has branches
in all the Provinces. A steady flow of reinforcements supplies the
wastage at the various fronts, and the labour required for
engineering, transport, etc., is now organised in 20 corps in
Mesopotamia and 25 corps in France. In addition 60,000 artisans,
labourers, and specialists are serving in Mesopotamia and East
Africa, and some 20,000 menials and followers have also gone
overseas. Indian medical practitioners have accepted temporary
commissions in the Indian Medical Service to the number of 500. In
view of this fact, due to Great Britain's bitter need of help, may we
not hope that this Service will welcome Indians in time of peace as
well as in time of war, and will no longer bar the way by
demanding the taking of a degree in the United Kingdom? It is also
worthy of notice that the I.M.S. officers in charge of district duties
have been largely replaced by Indian medical men; this, again,
should continue after the War. Another fact, that the Army Reserve
of Officers his risen from 40 to 2,000, suggests that the throwing
open of King's Commissions to qualified Indians should not be
represented by a meagre nine. If English lads of 19 and 20 are
worthy of King's Commissions—and the long roll of slain Second
Lieutenants proves it—then certainly Indian lads, since Indians

have fought as bravely as Englishmen, should find the door thrown open to them equally widely in their own country, and the Indian Army should be led by Indian officers.

With such a record of deeds as the one I have baldly sketched, it is not necessary to say much in words as to India's support of Great Britain and her Allies. She has proved up to the hilt her desire to remain within the Empire, to maintain her tie with Great Britain. But if Britain is to call successfully on India's man-power, as Lord Chelmsford suggests in his Man-Power Board, then must the man who fights or labours have a man's Rights in his own land. The lesson which springs out of this War is that it is absolutely necessary for the future safety of the Empire that India shall have Home Rule. Had her Man-Power been utilised earlier there would have been no War, for none would have dared to provoke Great Britain and India to a contest. But her Man-Power cannot be utilised while she is a subject Nation. She cannot afford to maintain a large army, if she is to support an English garrison, to pay for their goings and comings, to buy stores in England at exorbitant prices and send them back again when England needs them. She cannot afford to train men for England, and only have their services for five years. She cannot afford to keep huge Gold Reserves in England, and be straitened for cash, while she lends to England out of her Reserves, taken from her over-taxation, £27,000,000 for War expenses, and this, be it remembered, before the great War Loan. I once said in England: "The condition of India's loyalty is India's freedom." I may now add: "The condition of India's usefulness to the Empire is India's freedom." She will tax herself willingly when her taxes remain in the country and fertilise it, when they educate her people and thus increase their productive power, when they foster her trade and create for her new industries.

Great Britain needs India as much as India needs England, for prosperity in Peace as well as for safety in War. Mr. Montagu has wisely said that "for equipment in War a Nation needs freedom in Peace." Therefore I say that, for both countries alike, the lesson of the War is Home Rule for India.

Let me close this part of my subject by laying at the feet of His Imperial Majesty the loving homage of the thousands here assembled, with the hope and belief that, ere long, we shall lay there the willing and grateful homage of a free Nation.

CHAPTER II

CAUSES OF THE NEW SPIRIT IN INDIA

Apart from the natural exchange of thought between East and West, the influence of English education, literature and ideals, the effect of travel in Europe, Japan and the United States of America, and other recognised causes for the changed outlook in India, there have been special forces at work during the last few years to arouse a New Spirit in India, and to alter her attitude of mind. These may be summed up as:

(*a*) The Awakening of Asia.

(*b*) Discussions abroad on Alien Rule and Imperial Reconstruction.

(*c*) Loss of Belief in the Superiority of the White Races.

(*d*) The Awakening of Indian Merchants.

(*e*) The Awakening of Indian Womanhood to claim its Ancient Position.

(*f*) The Awakening of the Masses.

Each of these causes has had its share in the splendid change of attitude in the Indian Nation, in the uprising of a spirit of pride of country, of independence, of self-reliance, of dignity, of self-respect. The War has quickened the rate of evolution of the world, and no country has experienced the quickening more than our Motherland.

THE AWAKENING OF ASIA

In a conversation I had with Lord Minto, soon after his arrival as Viceroy, he discussed the so-called "unrest in India," and recognised it as the inevitable result of English Education, of English Ideals of Democracy, of the Japanese victory over Russia, and of the changing conditions in the outer world. I was therefore not surprised to read his remark that he recognised, "frankly and publicly, that new aspirations were stirring in the hearts of the people, that they were part of a larger movement common to the whole East, and that it was necessary to satisfy them to a reasonable extent by giving them a larger share in the administration."

But the present movement in India will be very poorly understood if it be regarded only in connexion with the movement in the East. The awakening of Asia is part of a world-movement, which has been quickened into marvellous rapidity by the world-war. The world-movement is towards Democracy, and for the West dates from the breaking away of the American Colonies from Great Britain, consummated in 1776, and its sequel in the French

Revolution of 1789. Needless to say that its root was in the growth of modern science, undermining the fabric of intellectual servitude, in the work of the Encyclopædists, and in that of Jean-Jacques Rousseau and of Thomas Paine. In the East, the swift changes in Japan, the success of the Japanese Empire against Russia, the downfall of the Manchu dynasty in China and the establishment of a Chinese Republic, the efforts at improvement in Persia, hindered by the interference of Russia and Great Britain with their growing ambitions, and the creation of British and Russian "spheres of influence," depriving her of her just liberty, and now the Russian Revolution and the probable rise of a Russian Republic in Europe and Asia, have all entirely changed the conditions before existing in India. Across Asia, beyond the Himalayas, stretch free and self-ruling Nations. India no longer sees as her Asian neighbours the huge domains of a Tsar and a Chinese despot, and compares her condition under British rule with those of their subject populations. British rule profited by the comparison, at least until 1905, when the great period of repression set in. But in future, unless India wins Self-Government, she will look enviously at her Self-Governing neighbours, and the contrast will intensify her unrest.

But even if she gains Home Rule, as I believe she will, her position in the Empire will imperatively demand that she shall be strong as well as free. She becomes not only a vulnerable point in the Empire, as the Asian Nations evolve their own ambitions and rivalries, but also a possession to be battled for. Mr. Laing once said: "India is the milch-cow of England," a Kamadhenu, in fact, a cow of plenty; and if that view should arise in Asia, the ownership of the milch-cow would become a matter of dispute, as of old between Vashishtha and Vishvamitra. Hence India must be capable of self-defence both by land and sea. There may be a struggle for the primacy of Asia, for supremacy in the Pacific, for the mastery of Australasia, to say nothing of the inevitable trade-struggles, in which Japan is already endangering Indian industry and Indian trade, while India is unable to protect herself.

In order to face these larger issues with equanimity, the Empire requires a contented, strong, self-dependent and armed India, able to hold her own and to aid the Dominions, especially Australia, with her small population and immense unoccupied and undefended area. India alone has the man-power which can effectively maintain the Empire in Asia, and it is a short-sighted, a criminally short-sighted, policy not to build up her strength as a Self-Governing State within the Commonwealth of Free Nations under the British Crown. The Englishmen in India talk loudly of their interests; what can this mere handful do to protect their interests against attack in the coming years? Only in a free and powerful India will they be safe. Those who read Japanese papers know how strongly, even during the War, they parade unchecked their pro-German sympathies, and how likely after the War is an alliance between these two ambitious and warlike Nations. Japan will come out of the War with her army and navy unweakened, and her trade immensely strengthened. Every consideration of sane statesmanship should lead Great Britain to trust India more than Japan, so that the British Empire in Asia may rest on the sure foundation of Indian loyalty, the loyalty of a free and contented people, rather than be dependent on the continued friendship of a possible future rival. For international friendships are governed by National interests, and are built on quicksands, not on rock.

Englishmen in India must give up the idea that English dominance is necessary for the protection of their interests, amounting, in 1915, to £365,399,000 sterling. They do not claim to dominate the United

States of America, because they have invested there £688,078,000. They do not claim to dominate the Argentine Republic, because they have invested there £269,808,000. Why then should they claim to dominate India on the ground of their investment? Britons must give up the idea that India is a possession to be exploited for their own benefit, and must see her as a friend, an equal, a Self-Governing Dominion within the Empire, a Nation like themselves, a willing partner in the Empire, and not a dependent. The democratic movement in Japan, China and Russia in Asia has sympathetically affected India, and it is idle to pretend that it will cease to affect her.

DISCUSSIONS ABROAD ON ALIEN RULE AND IMPERIAL RECONSTRUCTION

But there are other causes which have been working in India, consequent on the British attitude against autocracy and in defence of freedom in Europe, while her attitude to India has, until lately, been left in doubt. Therefore I spoke of a splendid opportunity lost. India at first believed whole-heartedly that Great Britain was fighting for the freedom of all Nationalities. Even now, Mr. Asquith declared—in his speech in the House of Commons reported here last October, on the peace resolution of Mr. Ramsay Macdonald— that "the Allies are fighting for nothing but freedom, and, an important addition—for nothing short of freedom." In his speech declaring that Britain would stand by France in her claim for the restoration of Alsace-Lorraine, he spoke of "the intolerable degradation of a foreign yoke." Is such a yoke less intolerable, less wounding to self-respect here, than in Alsace-Lorraine, where the rulers and the ruled are both of European blood, similar in religion and habits? As the War went on, India slowly and unwillingly came to realise that the hatred of autocracy was confined to autocracy in the West, and that the degradation was only regarded as intolerable for men of white races; that freedom was lavishly promised to all except to India; that new powers were to be given to the Dominions, but not to India. India was markedly left out of the speeches of statesmen dealing with the future of the Empire, and at last there was plain talk of the White Empire, the Empire of the Five Nations, and the "coloured races" were lumped together as the wards of the White Empire, doomed to an indefinite minority.

The peril was pressing; the menace unmistakable. The Reconstruction of the Empire was on the anvil; what was to be India's place therein? The Dominions were proclaimed as partners; was India to remain a Dependency? Mr. Bonar Law bade the Dominions strike while the iron was hot; was India to wait till it was cold? India saw her soldiers fighting for freedom in Flanders, in France, in Gallipoli, in Asia Minor, in China, in Africa; was she to have no share of the freedom for which she fought? At last she sprang to her feet and cried, in the words of one of her noblest sons: "Freedom is my birthright; and I want it." The words "Home Rule" became her Mantram. She claimed her place in the Empire.

Thus, while she continued to support, and even to increase, her army abroad, fighting for the Empire, and poured out her treasures as water for Hospital Ships, War Funds, Red Cross organisations, and the gigantic War Loan, a dawning fear oppressed her, lest, if she did not take order with her own household, success in the War for the Empire might mean decreased liberty for herself.

The recognition of the right of the Indian Government to make its voice heard in Imperial matters, when they were under discussion in an Imperial Conference, was a step in the right direction. But disappointment was felt that while other countries were represented by responsible Ministers, the representation in India's case was of the Government, of a Government irresponsible to her, and not the representative of herself. No fault was found with the choice itself, but only with the non-representative character of the chosen, for they were selected by the Government, and not by the elected members of the Supreme Council. This defect in the resolution moved by the Hon. Khan Bahadur M.M. Shafi on October 2, 1915, was pointed out by the Hon. Mr. Surendranath Bannerji. He said:

> My Lord, in view of a situation so full of hope and promise, it seems to me that my friend's Resolution does not go far enough. He pleads for official representation at the Imperial Conference: he does not plead for popular representation. He urges that an address be presented to His Majesty's Government, through the Secretary of State for India, for official representation at the Imperial Council. My Lord, official representation may mean little or nothing. It may indeed be attended with some risk; for I am sorry to have to say—but say it I must—that our officials do not always see eye to eye with us as regards many great public questions which affect this country; and indeed their views, judged from our standpoint, may sometimes seem adverse to our interests. At the same time, my Lord, I recognise the fact that the Imperial Conference is an assemblage of officials pure and simple, consisting of Ministers of the United Kingdom and of the self-governing

Colonies. But, my Lord, there is an essential difference between them and ourselves. In their case, the Ministers are the elect of the people, their organ and their voice, answerable to them for their conduct and their proceedings. In our case, our officials are public servants in name, but in reality they are the masters of the public. The situation may improve, and I trust it will, under the liberalising influence of your Excellency's beneficent administration; but we must take things as they are, and not indulge in building castles in the air, which may vanish "like the baseless fabric of a vision."

It was said to be an epoch-making event that "Indian Representatives" took part in the Conference. Representatives they were, but, as said, of the British Government in India, not of India, whereas their colleagues represented their Nations. They did good work, none the less, for they were able and experienced men, though they failed us in the Imperial Preference Conference and, partially, on the Indentured Labour question. Yet we hope that the presence in the Conference of men of Indian birth may prove to be the proverbial "thin end of the wedge," and may have convinced their colleagues that, while India was still a Dependency, India's sons were fully their equals.

The Report of the Public Services Commission, though now too obviously obsolete to be discussed, caused both disappointment and resentment; for it showed that, in the eyes of the majority of the Commissioners, English domination in Indian administration was to be perpetual, and that thirty years hence she would only hold a pitiful 25 per cent. or the higher appointments in the I.C.S. and the Police. I cannot, however, mention that Commission, even in passing, without voicing India's thanks to the Hon. Mr. Justice

Rahim, for his rare courage in writing a solitary Minute of Dissent, in which he totally rejected the Report, and laid down the right principles which should govern recruitment for the Indian Civil Services.

India had but three representatives on the Commission; G.K. Gokhale died ere it made its Report, his end quickened by his sufferings during its work, by the humiliation of the way in which his countrymen were treated. Of Mr. Abdur Rahim I have already spoken. The Hon. Mr. M.B. Chaubal signed the Report, but dissented from some of its most important recommendations. The whole Report was written "before the flood," and it is now merely an antiquarian curiosity.

India, for all these reasons, was forced to see before her a future of perpetual subordination: the Briton rules in Great Britain, the Frenchman in France, the American in America, each Dominion in its own area, but the Indian was to rule nowhere; alone among the peoples of the world, he was not to feel his own country as his own. "Britain for the British" was right and natural; "India for the Indians" was wrong, even seditious. It must be "India for the Empire," or not even for the Empire, but "for the rest of the Empire," careless of herself. "British support for British Trade" was patriotic and proper in Britain. "Swadeshi goods for Indians" showed a petty and anti-Imperial spirit in India. The Indian was to continue to live perpetually, and even thankfully, as Gopal Krishna Gokhale said he lived now, in "an atmosphere of inferiority," and to be proud to be a citizen (without rights) of the Empire, while its other component Nations were to be citizens (with rights) in their own countries first, and citizens of the Empire secondarily. Just as his trust in Great Britain was strained nearly to breaking point came the glad news of Mr. Montagu's appointment as Secretary of State for India, of the

Viceroy's invitation to him, and of his coming to hear for himself what India wanted. It was a ray of sunshine breaking through the gloom, confidence in Great Britain revived, and glad preparation was made to welcome the coming of a friend.

The attitude of India has changed to meet the changed attitude of the Governments of India and Great Britain. But let none imagine that that consequential change of attitude connotes any change in her determination to win Home Rule. She is ready to consider terms of peace, but it must be "peace with honour," and honour in this connection means Freedom. If this be not granted, an even more vigorous agitation will begin.

LOSS OF BELIEF IN THE SUPERIORITY OF WHITE RACES

The undermining of this belief dates from the spreading of the Arya Samaj and the Theosophical Society. Both bodies sought to lead the Indian people to a sense of the value of their own civilisation, to pride in their past, creating self-respect in the present, and self-confidence in the future. They destroyed the unhealthy inclination to imitate the West in all things, and taught discrimination, the using only of what was valuable in western thought and culture, instead of a mere slavish copying of everything. Another great force was that of Swami Vivekananda, alike in his passionate love and admiration for India, and his exposure of the evils resulting from Materialism in the West. Take the following:

Children of India, I am here to speak to you to-day about some practical things, and my object in reminding you about the glories of the past is simply this. Many times have I been told that looking into the past only degenerates and leads to nothing, and that we should look to the future. That is true. But out of the past is built the future. Look back, therefore, as far as you can, drink deep of the eternal fountains that are behind, and after that, look forward, march forward, and make India brighter, greater, much higher than she ever was. Our ancestors were great. We must recall that. We must learn the elements of our being, the blood that courses in our veins; we must have faith in that blood, and what it did in the past: and out of that faith, and consciousness of past greatness, we must build an India yet greater than what she has been.

And again:

I know for certain that millions, I say deliberately, millions, in every civilised land are waiting for the message that will save them from the hideous abyss of materialism into which modern money-worship is driving them headlong, and many of the leaders of the new Social Movements have already discovered that Vedanta in its highest form can alone spiritualise their social aspirations.

The process was continued by the admiration of Sanskrit literature expressed by European scholars and philosophers. But the effect of these was confined to the few and did not reach the many. The first great shock to the belief in white superiority came from the triumph of Japan over Russia, the facing of a huge European Power by a comparatively small Eastern Nation, the exposure of the weakness and rottenness of the Russian leaders, and the contrast with their hardy virile opponents, ready to sacrifice everything for their country.

The second great shock has come from the frank brutality of German theories of the State, and their practical carrying out in the treatment of conquered districts and the laying waste of evacuated areas in retreat. The teachings of Bismarck and their practical application in France, Flanders, Belgium, Poland, and Serbia have destroyed all the glamour of the superiority of Christendom over Asia. Its vaunted civilisation is seen to be but a thin veneer, and its religion a matter of form rather than of life. Gazing from afar at the ghastly heaps of dead and the hosts of the mutilated, at science turned into devilry and ever inventing new tortures for rending and slaying, Asia may be forgiven for thinking that, on the whole, she prefers her own religions and her own civilisations.

But even deeper than the outer tumult of war has pierced the doubt as to the reality of the Ideals of Liberty and Nationality so loudly proclaimed by the foremost western Nations, the doubt of the honesty of their champions. Sir James Meston said truly, a short time ago, that he had never, in his long experience, known Indians in so distrustful and suspicious a mood as that which he met in them to-day. And that is so. For long years Indians have been chafing over the many breaches of promises and pledges to them that remain unredeemed. The maintenance here of a system of political repression, of coercive measures increased in number and more harshly applied since 1905, the carrying of the system to a wider extent since the War for the sanctity of treaties and for the protection of Nationalities has been going on, have deepened the mistrust. A frank and courageous statesmanship applied to the honest carrying out of large reforms too long delayed can alone remove it. The time for political tinkering is past; the time for wise and definite changes is here.

To these deep causes must be added the comparison between the progressive policy of some of the Indian States in matters which most affect the happiness of the people, and the slow advance made under British administration. The Indian notes that this advance is made under the guidance of rulers and ministers of his own race. When he sees that the suggestions made in the People's Assembly in Mysore are fully considered and, when possible, given effect to, he realises that without the forms of power the members exercise more real power than those in our Legislative Councils. He sees education spreading, new industries fostered, villagers encouraged to manage their own affairs and take the burden of their own responsibility, and he wonders why Indian incapacity is so much more efficient than British capacity.

Perhaps, after all, for Indians, Indian rule may be the best.

THE AWAKENING OF THE MERCHANTS

THE AWAKENING OF INDIAN WOMANHOOD

The position of women in the ancient Aryan civilisation was a very noble one. The great majority married, becoming, as Manu said, the Light of the Home; some took up the ascetic life, remained

32

unmarried, and sought the knowledge of Brahma. The story of the Rani Damayanti, to whom her husband's ministers came, when they were troubled by the Raja's gambling, that of Gandhari, in the Council of Kings and Warrior Chiefs, remonstrating with her headstrong son; in later days, of Padmavati of Chitoor, of Mirabai of Marwar, the sweet poetess, of Tarabai of Thoda, the warrior, of Chand Bibi, the defender of Ahmednagar, of Ahalya Bai of Indore, the great Ruler—all these and countless others are well known.

Only in the last two or three generations have Indian women slipped away from their place at their husbands' side, and left them unhelped in their public life. But even now they wield great influence over husband and son. Culture has never forsaken them, but the English education of their husbands and sons, with the neglect of Sanskrit and the Vernacular, have made a barrier between the culture of the husband and that of the wife, and has shut the woman out from her old sympathy with the larger life of men. While the interests of the husband have widened, those of the wife have narrowed. The materialising of the husband tended also, by reaction, to render the wife's religion less broad and wise.

The wish to save their sons from the materialising results of English education awoke keen sympathy among Indian mothers with the movement to make religion an integral part of education. It was, perhaps, the first movement in modern days which aroused among them in all parts a keen and living interest.

The Partition of Bengal was bitterly resented by Bengali women, and was another factor in the outward-turning change. When the editor of an Extremist newspaper was prosecuted for sedition, convicted and sentenced, five hundred Bengali women went to his mother to show their sympathy, not by condolences, but by congratulations. Such was the feeling of the well-born women of Bengal.

Then the troubles of Indians outside India roused the ever quick sympathy of Indian women, and the attack in South Africa on the sacredness of Indian marriage drew large numbers of them out of their homes to protest against the wrong.

The Indentured Labour question, involving the dishonour of women, again, moved them deeply, and even sent a deputation to the Viceroy composed of women.

These were, perhaps, the chief outer causes; but deep in the heart of India's daughters arose the Mother's voice, calling on them to help Her to arise, and to be once more mistress in Her own household. Indian women, nursed on Her old literature, with its wonderful ideals of womanly perfection, could not remain indifferent to the great movement for India's liberty. And during the last few years the hidden fire, long burning in their hearts, fire of love to Bharatamata, fire of resentment against the lessened influence of the religion which they passionately love, instinctive dislike of the foreigner as ruling in their land, have caused a marvellous awakening. The strength of the Home Rule movement is rendered tenfold greater by the adhesion to it of large numbers of women, who bring to its helping the uncalculating heroism, the endurance, the self-sacrifice, of the feminine nature. Our League's best recruits are among the women of India, and the women of Madras boast that they marched in procession when the men were stopped, and that their prayers in the temples set the interned captives free. Home Rule has become so intertwined with religion by the prayers offered up in the great Southern Temples, sacred places of pilgrimage, and spreading from them to village temples, and also by its being preached up and down the country by Sadhus and Sannyasins, that it has become in the minds of the women and of the ever religious masses, inextricably intertwined with religion. That is, in this country, the surest way of winning alike the women of the higher classes and the men and women villagers. And that is why I have said that the two words, "Home Rule," have become a Mantram.

THE AWAKENING OF THE MASSES

CHAPTER III

WHY INDIA DEMANDS HOME RULE

India demands Home Rule for two reasons, one essential and vital, the other less important but necessary: Firstly, because Freedom is the birthright of every Nation; secondly, because her most important interests are now made subservient to the interests of the British Empire without her consent, and her resources are not utilised for her greatest needs. It is enough only to mention the money spent on her Army, not for local defence but for Imperial purposes, as compared with that spent on primary education.

I

THE VITAL REASON

What is a Nation?

Self-Government is necessary to the self-respect and dignity of a People; Other-Government emasculates a Nation, lowers its character, and lessens its capacity. The wrong done by the Arms Act, which Raja Rampal Singh voiced in the Second Congress as a wrong which outweighed all the benefits of British Rule, was its weakening and debasing effect on Indian manhood. "We cannot," he declared, "be grateful to it for degrading our natures, for systematically crushing out all martial spirit, for converting a race of soldiers and heroes into a timid flock of quill-driving sheep." This was done not by the fact that a man did not carry arms—few carry them in England—but that men were deprived of the right to carry them. A Nation, an individual, cannot develop his capacities to the utmost without liberty. And this is recognised everywhere except in India. As Mazzini truly said:

God has written a line of His thought over the cradle of

every people. That is its special mission. It cannot be cancelled; it must be freely developed.

For what is a Nation? It is a spark of the Divine Fire, a fragment of the Divine Life, outbreathed into the world, and gathering round itself a mass of individuals, men, women and children, whom it binds together into one. Its qualities, its powers, in a word, its type, depend on the fragment of the Divine Life embodied in it, the Life which shapes it, evolves it, colours it, and makes it One. The magic of Nationality is the feeling of oneness, and the use of Nationality is to serve the world in the particular way for which its type fits it. This is what Mazzini called "its special mission," the duty given to it by God in its birth-hour. Thus India had the duty of spreading the idea of Dharma, Persia that of Purity, Egypt that of Science, Greece that of Beauty, Rome that of Law. But to render its full service to Humanity it must develop along its own lines, and be Self-determined in its evolution. It must be Itself, and not Another. The whole world suffers where a Nationality is distorted or suppressed, before its mission to the world is accomplished.

The Cry for Self-Rule

Hence the cry of a Nation for Freedom, for Self-Rule, is not a cry of mere selfishness demanding more Rights that it may enjoy more happiness. Even in that there is nothing wrong, for happiness means fulness of life, and to enjoy such fulness is a righteous claim.

But the demand for Self-Rule is a demand for the evolution of its own nature for the Service of Humanity. It is a demand of the deepest Spirituality, an expression of the longing to give its very best to the world. Hence dangers cannot check it, nor threats appal, nor offerings of greater pleasures lure it to give up its demand for Freedom. In the adapted words of a Christian Scripture, it passionately cries: "What shall it profit a Nation if it gain the whole world and lose its own Soul? What shall a Nation give in exchange for its Soul?" Better hardship and freedom, than luxury and thraldom. This is the spirit of the Home Rule movement, and therefore it cannot be crushed, it cannot be destroyed, it is eternal and ever young. Nor can it be persuaded to exchange its birthright for any mess of efficiency-pottage at the hands of the bureaucracy.

Stunting the Race

Coming closer to the daily life of the people as individuals, we see that the character of each man, woman and child is degraded and weakened by a foreign administration, and this is most keenly felt by the best Indians. Speaking on the employment of Indians in the Public Services, Gopal Krishna Gokhale said:

A kind of dwarfing or stunting of the Indian race is going on under the present system. We must live all the days of our life in an atmosphere of inferiority, and the tallest of us must bend, in order that the exigencies of the system may be satisfied. The upward impulse, if I may use such an expression, which every schoolboy at Eton or Harrow may feel that he may one day be a Gladstone, a Nelson, or a Wellington, and which may draw forth the best efforts of which he is capable, that is denied to us. The full height to which our manhood is capable of rising can never be reached by us under the present system. The moral elevation which every Self-governing people feel cannot be felt by us. Our administrative and military talents must gradually disappear owing to sheer disuse, till at last our lot, as hewers of wood and drawers of water in our own country, is stereotyped.

The Hon. Mr. Bhupendranath Basu has spoken on similar lines:

A bureaucratic administration, conducted by an imported agency, and centring all power in its hands, and undertaking all responsibility, has acted as a dead weight on the Soul of India, stifling in us all sense of initiative, for the lack of which we are condemned, atrophying the nerves of action and, what is more serious, necessarily dwarfing in us all feeling of self-respect.

In this connexion the warning of Lord Salisbury to Cooper's Hill students is significant:

No system of Government can be permanently safe where there is a feeling of inferiority or of mortification affecting the relations between the governing and the governed. There is nothing I would more earnestly wish to impress upon all who leave this country for the purpose of governing India than that, if they choose to be so, they are the only enemies England has to fear. They are the persons

40

who can, if they will, deal a blow of the deadliest character
at the future rule of England.

I have ventured to urge this danger, which has increased of late years, in consequence of the growing self-respect of the Indians, but the ostrich policy is thought to be preferable in my part of the country.

This stunting of the race begins with the education of the child. The Schools differentiate between British and Indian teachers; the Colleges do the same. The students see first-class Indians superseded by young and third-rate foreigners; the Principal of a College should be a foreigner; foreign history is more important than Indian; to have written on English villages is a qualification for teaching economics in India; the whole atmosphere of the School and College emphasises the superiority of the foreigner, even when the professors abstain from open assertion thereof. The Education Department controls the education given, and it is planned on foreign models, and its object is to serve foreign rather than native ends, to make docile Government servants rather than patriotic citizens; high spirits, courage, self-respect, are not encouraged, and docility is regarded as the most precious quality in the student; pride in country, patriotism, ambition, are looked on as dangerous, and English, instead of Indian, Ideals are exalted; the blessings of a foreign rule and the incapacity of Indians to manage their own affairs are constantly inculcated. What wonder that boys thus trained often turn out, as men, time-servers and sycophants, and, finding their legitimate ambitions frustrated, become selfish and care little for the public weal? Their own inferiority has been so driven into them during their most impressionable years, that they do not even feel what Mr. Asquith called the "intolerable degradation of a foreign yoke."

India's Rights

It is not a question whether the rule is good or bad. German efficiency in Germany is far greater than English efficiency in England; the Germans were better fed, had more amusements and leisure, less crushing poverty than the English. But would any Englishman therefore desire to see Germans occupying all the highest positions in England? Why not? Because the righteous self-respect and dignity of the free man revolt against foreign domination, however superior. As Mr. Asquith said at the beginning of the War, such a condition was "inconceivable and would be intolerable." Why then is it the one conceivable system here in India? Why is it not felt by all Indians to be intolerable? It is because it has become a habit, bred in us from childhood, to regard the sahib-log as our natural superiors, and the greatest injury British rule has done to Indians is to deprive them of the natural instinct born in all free peoples, the feeling of an inherent right to Self-determination, to be themselves. Indian dress, Indian food, Indian ways, Indian customs, are all looked on as second-rate; Indian mother-tongue and Indian literature cannot make an educated man. Indians as well as Englishmen take it for granted that the natural rights of every Nation do not belong to them; they claim "a larger share in the government of the country," instead of claiming the government of their own country, and they are expected to feel grateful for "," for concessions. Britain is to say what she will give. The whole thing is wrong, topsy-turvy, irrational. Thank God that India's eyes are opening; that myriads of her people realise that they are men, with a man's right to freedom in his own country, a man's right to manage his own affairs. India is no longer on her knees for boons; she is on her feet for Rights. It is because I have taught this that the English in India misunderstand me and call me seditious; it is because I have taught this that I am President of this Congress to-day.

This may seem strong language, because the plain truth is not usually put in India. But this is what every Briton feels in Britain for his own country, and what every Indian should feel in India for his. This is the Freedom for which the Allies are fighting; this is Democracy, the Spirit of the Age. And this is what every true Briton will feel is India's Right the moment India claims it for herself, as she is claiming it now. When this right is gained, then will the tie between India and Great Britain become a golden link of mutual love and service, and the iron chain of a foreign yoke will fall away. We shall live and work side by side, with no sense of distrust and dislike, working as brothers for common ends. And from that union shall arise the mightiest Empire, or rather Commonwealth, that the world has ever known, a Commonwealth that, in God's good time, shall put an end to War.

II

THE SECONDARY REASONS

Tests of Efficiency

The Secondary Reasons for the present demand for Home Rule may be summed up in the blunt statement: "The present rule, while efficient in less important matters and in those which concern British interests, is inefficient in the greater matters on which the healthy life and happiness of the people depend." Looking at outer things, such as external order, posts and telegraphs—except where political agitators are concerned—main roads, railways, etc., foreign visitors, who expected to find a semi-savage country, hold up their hands in admiration. But if they saw the life of the people, the masses of struggling clerks trying to educate their children on Rs. 25 (28s. 0-1/4d.) a month, the masses of labourers with one meal a day, and the huts in which they live, they would find cause for thought. And if the educated men talked freely with them, they

44

would be surprised at their bitterness. Gopal Krishna Gokhale put the whole matter very plainly in 1911:

> One of the fundamental conditions of the peculiar position of the British Government in this country is that it should be a continuously progressive Government. I think all thinking men, to whatever community they belong, will accept that. Now, I suggest four tests to judge whether the Government is progressive, and, further, whether it is continuously progressive. The first test that I would apply is what measures it adopts for the moral and material improvement of the mass of the people, and under these measures I do not include those appliances of modern Governments which the British Government has applied in this country, because they were appliances necessary for its very existence, though they have benefited the people, such as the construction of Railways, the introduction of Post and Telegraphs, and things of that kind. By measures for the moral and material improvement of the people, I mean what the Government does for education, what the Government does for sanitation, what the Government does for agricultural development, and so forth. That is my first test. The second test that I would apply is what steps the Government takes to give us a larger share in the administration of our local affairs—in municipalities and local boards. My third test is what voice the Government gives us in its Councils—in those deliberate assemblies, where policies are considered. And, lastly, we must consider how far Indians are admitted into the ranks of the public service.

A Change of System Needed

Those were Gokhale's tests, and Indians can supply the results of their knowledge and experience to answer them. But before dealing with the failure to meet these tests, it is necessary to state here that it is not a question of blaming men, or of substituting Indians for Englishmen, but of changing the system itself. It is a commonplace that the best men become corrupted by the possession of irresponsible power. As Bernard Houghton says: "The possession of unchecked power corrupts some of the finer qualities." Officials quite honestly come to believe that those who try to change the system are undermining the security of the State. They identify the State with themselves, so that criticism of them is seen as treason to the State. The phenomenon is well known in history, and it is only repeating itself in India. The same writer—I prefer to use his words rather than my own, for he expresses exactly my own views, and will not be considered to be prejudiced as I am thought to be—cogently remarks:

> He (the official) has become an expert in reports and returns and matters of routine through many years of practice. They are the very woof and warp of his brain. He has no ideas, only reflexes. He views with acrid disfavour untried conceptions. From being constantly preoccupied with the manipulation of the machine he regards its smooth working, the ordered and harmonious regulation of glittering pieces of machinery, as the highest service he can render to the country of his adoption. He determines that his particular cog-wheel at least shall be bright, smooth, silent, and with absolutely no back-lash. Not

unnaturally in course of time he comes to envisage the world through the strait embrasure of an office window. When perforce he must report on new proposals he will place in the forefront, not their influence on the life and progress of the people, but their convenience to the official hierarchy and the manner in which they affect its authority. Like the monks of old, or the squire in the typical English village, he cherishes a benevolent interest in the commonalty, and is quite willing, even eager, to take a general interest in their welfare, if only they do not display initiative or assert themselves in opposition to himself or his order. There is much in this proviso. Having come to regard his own judgment as almost divine, and the hierarchy of which he has the honour to form a part as a sacrosanct institution, he tolerates the laity so long as they labour quietly and peaceably at their vocations and do not presume to inter-meddle in high matters of State. That is the heinous offence. And frank criticism of official acts touches a lower depth still, even lèse majesté. For no official will endure criticism from his subordinates, and the public, who lie in outer darkness beyond the pale, do not in his estimation rank even with his subordinates. How, then, should he listen with patience when in their cavilling way they insinuate that, in spite of the labours of a high-souled bureaucracy, all is perhaps not for the best in the best of all possible worlds—still less when they suggest reforms that had never occurred even to him or to his order, and may clash with his most cherished ideals? It is for the officials to govern the country; they alone have been initiated into the sacred mysteries; they alone understand the secret working of the machine. At the utmost the laity may tender respectful and humble suggestions for their consideration, but no more. As for those who dare to think and act for themselves, their ignorant folly is only equalled by their arrogance. It is as though a handful of schoolboys were to dictate to their masters alterations in the traditional time-table, or to insist on a modified curriculum.... These worthy people [officials] confuse manly independence with disloyalty; they cannot conceive of natives except either as rebels or as timid sheep.

Non-Official Anglo-Indians

The problem becomes more complicated by the existence in India of a small but powerful body of the same race as the higher officials; there are only 122,919 English-born persons in this country, while there are 245,000,000 in the British Raj and another 70,000,000 in the Indian States, more or less affected by British influence. As a rule, the non-officials do not take any part in politics, being otherwise occupied; but they enter the field when any hope arises in Indian hearts of changes really beneficial to the Nation. John Stuart Mill observed on this point:

The individuals of the ruling people who resort to the foreign country to make their fortunes are of all others

48

those who most need to be held under powerful restraint. They are always one of the chief difficulties of the Government. Armed with the prestige and filled with the scornful overbearingness of the conquering Nation, they have the feelings inspired by absolute power without its sense of responsibility.

Similarly, Sir John Lawrence wrote:

The difficulty in the way of the Government of India acting fairly in these matters is immense. If anything is done, or attempted to be done, to help the natives, a general howl is raised, which reverberates in England, and finds sympathy and support there. I feel quite bewildered sometimes what to do. Everyone is, in the abstract, for justice, moderation, and suchlike excellent qualities; but when one comes to apply such principles so as to affect anybody's interests, then a change comes over them.

Keene, speaking of the principle of treating equally all classes of the community, says:

The application of that maxim, however, could not be made without sometimes provoking opposition among the handful of white settlers in India who, even when not connected with the administration, claimed a kind of class ascendancy which was not only in the conditions of the country but also in the nature of the case. It was perhaps natural that in a land of caste the compatriots of the rulers should become—as Lord Lytton said—a kind of "white Brahmanas"; and it was certain that, as a matter of fact, the pride of race and the possession of western civilisation created a sense of superiority, the display of which was ungraceful and even dangerous, when not tempered by official responsibility. This feeling had been sensitive enough in the days of Lord William Bentinck, when the class referred to was small in numbers and devoid of influence. It was now both more numerous, and—by reason of its connection with the newspapers of Calcutta and of London—it was far better able to make its passion heard.

During Lord Ripon's sympathetic administration the great outburst occurred against the Ilbert Bill in 1883. We are face to face with a similar phenomenon to-day, when we see the European Associations—under the leadership of the Madras Mail, the Englishman of Calcutta, the Pioneer of Allahabad, the Civil and Military Gazette of Lahore, with their Tory and Unionist allies in the London Press and with the aid of retired Indian officials and non-officials in England—desperately resisting the Reforms now proposed. Their opposition, we know, is a danger to the movement towards Freedom, and even when they have failed to impress England—as they are evidently failing—they will try to minimise or smother here the reforms which a statute has embodied. The Minto-Morley reforms were thus robbed of their usefulness, and a similar attempt, if not guarded against, will be made when the Congress-League Scheme is used as the basis for an Act.

The Re-action on England

We cannot leave out of account here the deadly harm done to England herself by this un-English system of rule in India. Mr. Hobson has pointed out:

As our free Self-Governing Colonies have furnished hope, encouragement, and leading to the popular aspirations in Great Britain, not merely by practical success in the art of Self-Government, but by the wafting of a spirit of freedom and equality, so our despotically ruled Dependencies have ever served to damage the character of our people by feeding the habits of snobbish subservience, the admiration of wealth and rank, the corrupt survivals of the inequalities of feudalism.... Cobden writing in 1860 of our Indian Empire, put this pithy question: "Is it not just possible that we may become corrupted at home by the reaction of arbitrary political maxims in the East upon our domestic politics, just as Greece and Rome were demoralised by their contact with Asia?" Not merely is the reaction possible, it is inevitable. As the despotic portion of our Empire, has grown in area, a large number of men, trained in the temper and methods of autocracy, as soldiers and civil officials in our Crown Colonies, Protectorates and Indian Empire, reinforced by numbers of merchants, planters, engineers, and overseers, whose lives have been those of a superior caste living an artificial life removed from all the healthy restraints of ordinary European Society, have returned to this country, bringing back the characters, sentiments and ideas imposed by this foreign environment.

It is a little hard on the I.C.S. that they should be foreigners here, and then, when they return to their native land, find that they have become foreigners there by the corrupting influences with which they are surrounded here. We import them as raw material to our own disadvantage, and when we export them as manufactured here, Great Britain and India alike suffer from their reactionary tendencies. The results are unsatisfactory to both sides.

The First Test Applied

Let us now apply Gokhale's first test. What has the Bureaucracy done for "education, sanitation, agricultural improvement, and so forth"? I must put the facts very briefly, but they are indisputable.

Education. The percentage to the whole population of children receiving education is 2.8, the percentage having risen by 0.9 since Mr. Gokhale moved his Education Bill six years ago. The percentage of children of school-going age attending school is 18.7. In 1913 the Government of India put the number of pupils at 4-1/2 millions; this has been accomplished in 63 years, reckoning from Sir Charles Wood's Educational Despatch in 1854, which led to the formation of the Education Department. In 1870 an Education Act was passed in Great Britain, the condition of Education in England then much resembling our present position; grants-in-aid in England had been given since 1833, chiefly to Church Schools. Between 1870 and 1881 free and compulsory education was established, and in 12 years the attendance rose from 43.3 to nearly 100 per cent. There are now 6,000,000 children in the schools of England and Wales out of a population of 40 millions. Japan, before 1872, had a proportion of 28 per cent. of children of school-going age in school, nearly 10 over our present proportion; in 24 years the percentage was raised to 92, and in 28 years education was free and compulsory. In Baroda education is free and largely compulsory and the percentage of boys is 100 per cent. Travancore has 81.1 per cent. of boys and 33.2 of girls. Mysore has 45.8 of boys and 9.7 of girls. Baroda spends an. 6-6 per head on school-going children, British India one anna. Expenditure on education advanced between 1882 and 1907 by 57 lakhs. Land-revenue had increased by 8 crores, military expenditure by 13 crores, civil by 8 crores, and capital outlay on railways was 15 crores. (I am quoting G.K. Gokhale's figures.) He ironically calculated that, if the population did not increase, every boy would be in school 115 years hence, and every girl in 665 years. Brother Delegates, we hope to do it more quickly under Home Rule. I submit that in Education the Bureaucracy is inefficient.

Sanitation and Medical Relief. The prevalence of plague, cholera, and above all malaria, shows the lack of sanitation alike in town and country. This lack is one of the causes contributing to the low average life-period in India—23.5 years. In England the life-period is 40 years, in New Zealand 60. The chief difficulty in the way of the treatment of disease is the encouragement of the foreign system of medicine, especially in rural parts, and the withholding of grants from the indigenous. Government Hospitals, Government Dispensaries, Government doctors, must all be on the foreign system. Ayurvaidic and Unani medicines, Hospitals, Dispensaries, Physicians, are unrecognised, and to "cover" the latter is "infamous" conduct. Travancore gives grants-in-aid to 72 Vaidyashalas, at which 143,505 patients—22,000 more than in allopathic institutions—were treated in 1914-15 (the Report issued in 1917). Our Government cannot grapple with the medical needs of the people, yet will not allow the people's money to be spent on the systems they prefer. Under Home Rule the indigenous and the foreign systems will be treated with impartiality. I grant that the allopathic doctors do their utmost to supply the need, and show great self-sacrifice, but the need is too vast and the numbers too few. Efficiency on their own lines in this matter is therefore impossible for our bureaucratic Government; their fault lies in excluding the indigenous systems, which they have not condescended to examine before rejecting them. The result is that in sanitation and medical relief the Bureaucracy is inefficient.

Agricultural Development. The census of 1911 gives the agricultural population at 218.3 millions. Its frightful poverty is a matter of common knowledge; its ever-increasing load of indebtedness has been dwelt on for at least the last thirty odd years by Sir Dinshaw E. Wacha. Yet the increasing debt is accompanied with increasing taxation, land revenue having risen, as just stated, in 25 years, by 8 crores—80,000,000—of rupees. In addition to this there are local cesses, salt tax, etc. The salt tax, which presses most hardly on the very poor, was raised in the last budget by Rs. 9 millions. The inevitable result of this poverty is malnutrition, resulting in low vitality, lack of resistance to disease, short life-period, huge infantile mortality. Gopal Krishna Gokhale, no mischievous agitator, repeated in 1905 the figures; often quoted:

Forty millions of people, according to one great Anglo-Indian authority—Sir William Hunter—pass through life with only one meal a day. According to another authority—Sir Charles Elliot—70 millions of people in India do not know what it is to have their hunger fully satisfied even once in the whole course of the year. The poverty of the people of India, thus considered by itself, is truly appalling. And if this is the state of things after a hundred years of your rule, you cannot claim that your principal aim in India has been the promotion of the interests of the Indian people.

It is sometimes said: "Why harp on these figures? We know them." Our answer is that the fact is ever harping in the stomach of the people, and while it continues we cannot cease to draw attention to it. And Gokhale urged that "even this deplorable condition has been further deteriorating steadily." We have no figures on malnutrition among the peasantry, but in Madras City, among an equally poor urban population, we found that 78 per cent. of our pupils were reported, after a medical inspection, to be suffering from malnutrition. And the spareness of frame, the thinness of arms and legs, the pitiably weak grip on life, speak without words to the seeing eye. It needs an extraordinary lack of imagination not to suffer while these things are going on.

The peasants' grievances are many and have been voiced year after year by this Congress. The Forest Laws, made by legislators inappreciative of village difficulties, press hardly on them, and only in a small number of places have Forest Panchayats been established. In the few cases in which the experiment has been made the results have been good, in some cases marvellously good. The paucity of grazing grounds for their cattle, the lack of green manure to feed their impoverished lands, the absence of fencing round forests, so that the cattle stray in when feeding, are impounded, and have to be redeemed, the fines and other punishments imposed for offences ill-understood, the want of wood for fuel, for tools, for repairs, the uncertain distribution of the available water, all these troubles are discussed in villages and in local Conferences. The Arms Act oppresses them, by leaving them defenceless against wild beasts and wild men. The union of Judicial and Executive functions makes justice often inaccessible, and always costly both in money and in time. The village officials naturally care more to please the Tahsildar and the Collector than the villagers, to whom they are in no way responsible. And factions flourish, because there is always a third party to whom to resort, who may be flattered if his rank be high, bribed if it be low, whose favour can be gained in either case by cringing and by subservience and tale-bearing. As regards the condition of agriculture in India and the poverty of the agricultural population, the Bureaucracy is inefficient.

The application of Mr. Gokhale's first test to Indian handicrafts, to the strengthening of weak industries and the creation of new, to the care of waterways for traffic and of the coast transport shipping, the protection of indigo and other indigenous dyes against their German synthetic rivals, etc., would show similar answers. We are suffering now from the supineness of the Bureaucracy as regards the development of the resources of the country, by its careless indifference to the usurping by Germans of some of those resources, and even now they are pursuing a similar policy of laissez faire towards Japanese enterprise, which, leaning on its own Government, is taking the place of Germany in shouldering Indians out of their own natural heritage.

In all prosperous countries crafts are found side by-side with agriculture, and they lend each other mutual support. The extreme poverty of Ireland, and the loss of more than half its population by emigration, were the direct results of the destruction of its wool-industry by Great Britain, and the consequent throwing of the population entirely on the land for subsistence. A similar phenomenon has resulted here from a similar case, but on a far more widespread scale. And here, a novel and portentous change for India, "a considerable landless class is developing, which involves economic danger," as the Imperial Gazeteer remarks, comparing the census returns of 1891 and 1901. "The ordinary agricultural labourers are employed on the land only during the busy seasons of the year, and in slack times a few are attracted to large trade-centres for temporary work." One recalls the influx into England of Irish labourers at harvest time. Professor Radkamal Mukerji has laid stress on the older conditions of village life. He says:

> The village is still almost self-sufficing, and is in itself an economic unit. The village agriculturist grows all the food necessary for the inhabitants of the village. The smith makes the plough-shares for the cultivator, and the few iron utensils required for the household. He supplies these to the people, but does not get money in return. He is recompensed by mutual services from his fellow villagers. The potter supplies him with pots, the weaver with cloth, and the oilman with oil. From the cultivator each of these artisans receives his traditional share of grain. Thus almost all the economic transactions are carried on without the use of money. To the villagers money is only a store of value, not a medium of exchange. When they happen to be rich in money, they hoard it either in coins or make ornaments made of gold and silver.

These conditions are changing in consequence of the pressure of poverty driving the villagers to the city, where they learn to substitute the competition of the town for the mutual helpfulness of the village. The difference of feeling, the change from trustfulness to suspicion, may be seen by visiting villages which are in the vicinity of a town and comparing their villagers with those who inhabit villages in purely rural areas. This economic and moral deterioration can only be checked by the re-establishment of a healthy and interesting village life, and this depends upon the re-establishment of the Panchayat as the unit of Government, a question which I deal with presently. Village industries would then revive and an intercommunicating network would be formed by Co-operative Societies. Mr. C.P. Ramaswami Aiyar says in his pamphlet, Co-operative Societies and Panchayats:

> The one method by which this evil [emigration to towns] can be arrested and the economic and social standards of life of the rural people elevated is by the inauguration of healthy Panchayats in conjunction with the foundation of Co-operative institutions, which will have the effect of resuscitating village industries, and of creating organised social forces. The Indian village, when rightly reconstructed, would be an excellent foundation for well-developed co-operative industrial organisation.

Again:

> The resuscitation of the village system has other bearings, not usually considered in connection with the general subject of the inauguration of the Panchayat system. One of the most important of these is the regeneration of the small industries of the land. Both in Europe and in India

the decline of small industries has gone on pari passu with the decline of farming on a small scale. In countries like France agriculture has largely supported village industries, and small cultivators in that country have turned their attention to industry as a supplementary source of livelihood. The decline of village life in India is not only a political, but also an economic and industrial, problem. Whereas in Europe the cultural impulse has travelled from the city to the village, in India the reverse has been the case. The centre of social life in this country is the village, and not the town. Ours was essentially the cottage industry, and our artisans still work in their own huts, more or less out of touch with the commercial world. Throughout the world the tendency has been of late to lay considerable emphasis on distributive and industrial co-operation based on a system of village industries and enterprise. Herein would be found the origins of the arts and crafts guilds and the Garden Cities, the idea underlying all these being to inaugurate a reign of Socialism and Co-operation, eradicating the entirely unequal distribution of wealth amongst producers and consumers. India has always been a country of small tenantry, and has thereby escaped many of the evils the western Nations have experienced owing to the concentration of wealth in a few hands. The communistic sense in our midst, and the fundamental tenets of our family life, have checked such concentration of capital. This has been the cause for the non-development of factory industries on a large scale.

The need for these changes—to which England is returning, after full experience of the miseries of life in manufacturing towns—is pressing.

Addressing an English audience, G.K. Gokhale summed up the general state of India as follows:

> Your average annual income has been estimated at about £42 per head. Ours, according to official estimates, is about £2 per head, and according to non-official estimates, only a little more than £1 per head. Your imports per head are about £13: ours about 5s. per head. The total deposits in your Postal Savings Bank amount to 148 million sterling, and you have in addition in the Trustees' Savings Banks about 52 million sterling. Our Postal Savings Bank deposits, with a population seven times as large as yours, are only about 7 million sterling, and even of this a little over one-tenth is held by Europeans. Your total paid-up capital of joint-stock companies is about 1,900 million sterling. Ours is not quite 26 million sterling, and the greater part of this again is European. Four-fifths of our people are dependent upon agriculture, and agriculture has been for some time steadily deteriorating. Indian agriculturists are too poor, and are, moreover, too heavily indebted, to be able to apply any capital to land, and the result is that over the greater part of India agriculture is, as Sir James Caird pointed out more than twenty-five years ago, only a process of exhaustion of the soil. The yield per acre is steadily diminishing, being now only about 8 to 9 bushels an acre against about 30 bushels here in England.

In all the matters which come under Gokhale's first test, the Bureaucracy has been and is inefficient.

Give Indians a Chance

All we say in the matter is: You have not succeeded in bringing education, health, prosperity, to the masses of the people. Is it not time to give Indians a chance of doing, for their own country, work similar to that which Japan and other nations have done for theirs? Surely the claim is not unreasonable. If the Anglo-Indians say that the masses are their peculiar care, and that the educated classes care not for them, but only for place and power, then we point to the Congress, to the speeches and the resolutions eloquent of their love and their knowledge. It is not their fault that they gaze on their country's poverty in helpless despair. Or let Mr. Justice Rahim answer:

As for the representation of the interests of the many scores of millions in India, if the claim be that they are better represented by European Officials than by educated Indian Officials or non-Officials, it is difficult to conceive how such reckless claim has come to be urged. The inability of English Officials to master the spoken language of India and their habits of life and modes of thought so completely divide them from the general population, that only an extremely limited few, possessed with extraordinary powers of insight, have ever been able to surmount the barriers. With the educated Indians, on the other hand, this knowledge is instinctive, and the view of religion and custom so strong in the East make their knowledge and sympathy more real than is to be seen in countries dominated by materialistic conceptions.

And it must be remembered that it is not lack of ability which has brought about bureaucratic inefficiency, for British traders and producers have done uncommonly well for themselves in India. But a Bureaucracy does not trouble itself about matters of this kind; the Russian Bureaucracy did not concern itself with the happiness of the Russian masses, but with their obedience and their paying of taxes. Bureaucracies are the same everywhere, and therefore it is the system we wage war upon, not the men; we do not want to substitute Indian bureaucrats for British bureaucrats; we want to abolish Bureaucracy, Government by Civil Servants.

The Other Tests Applied

I need not delay over the second, third, and fourth tests, for the answers sautent aux yeux.

The second test, Local Self-Government: Under Lord Mayo (1869-72) some attempts were made at decentralisation, called by Keene "Home Rule" (!), and his policy was followed on non-financial lines as well by Lord Ripon, who tried to infuse into what Keene calls "the germs of Home Rule" "the breath of life." Now, in 1917, an experimental and limited measure of local Home Rule is to be tried in Bengal. Though the Report of the Decentralisation Committee was published in 1909, we have not yet arrived at the universal election of non-official Chairmen. Decidedly inefficient is the Bureaucracy under test 2.

The third test, Voice in the Councils: The part played by Indian elected members in the Legislative Council, Madras, was lately described by a member as "a farce." The Supreme Legislative Council was called by one of its members "a glorified Debating Society." A table of resolutions proposed by Indian elected members, and passed or lost, was lately drawn up, and justified the caustic epithets. With regard to the Minto-Morley reforms, the Bureaucracy showed great efficiency in destroying the benefits intended by the Parliamentary Statute. But the third test shows that in giving Indians a fair voice in the Councils the Bureaucracy was inefficient.

The fourth test, the Admission of Indians to the Public Services: This is shown, by the Report of the Commission, not to need any destructive activity on the part of the Bureaucracy to prove their unwillingness to pass it, for the Report protects them in their privileged position.

We may add to Gokhale's tests one more, which will be triumphantly passed, the success of the Bureaucracy in increasing the cost of administration. The estimates for the revenue of the coming year stand at £86,199,600 sterling. The expenditure is reckoned at £85,572,100 sterling. The cost of administration stands at more than half the total revenue:

Civil Departments Salaries and Expenses	£19,323,300
Civil Miscellaneous Charges	5,283,300
Military Services	23,165,900
	£47,772,500

The reduction of the abnormal cost of government in India is of the most pressing nature, but this will never be done until we win Home Rule.

It will be seen that the Secondary Reasons for the demand for Home Rule are of the weightiest nature in themselves, and show the necessity for its grant if India is to escape from a poverty which threatens to lead to National bankruptcy, as it has already led to a short life-period and a high death rate, to widespread disease, and to a growing exhaustion of the soil. That some radical change must be brought about in the condition of our masses, if a Revolution of Hunger is to be averted, is patent to all students of history, who also know the poverty of the Indian masses to-day. This economic condition is due to many causes, of which the inevitable lack of understanding by an alien Government is only one. A system of government suitable to the West was forced on the East, destroying its own democratic and communal institutions and imposing bureaucratic methods which bewildered and deteriorated a people to whom they were strange and repellent. The result is not a matter for recrimination, but for change. An inappropriate system forced on an already highly civilised people was bound to fail. It has been rightly said that the poor only revolt when the misery they are enduring is greater than the dangers of revolt. We need Home Rule to stop the daily suffering of our millions from the diminishing yield of the soil and the decay of village industries.

THE BASIS OF MORALITY

I

REVELATION

Must religion and morals go together? Can one be taught without the other? It is a practical question for educationists, and France tried to answer it in the dreariest little cut and dry kind of catechism ever given to boys to make them long to be wicked. But apart from education, the question of the bedrock on which morals rest, the foundation on which a moral edifice can be built that will stand secure against the storms of life—that is a question of perennial interest, and it must be answered by each of us, if we would have a test of Right and Wrong, would know why Right is Right, why Wrong is Wrong.

Religions based on Revelation find in Revelation their basis for morality, and for them that is Right which the Giver of the Revelation commands, and that is Wrong which He forbids. Right is Right because God, or a Rṣhi or a Prophet, commands it, and Right rests on the Will of a Lawgiver, authoritatively revealed in a Scripture.

Now all Revelation has two great disadvantages as a basis for morality. It is fixed, and therefore unprogressive; while man evolves, and at a later stage of his growth, the morality taught in the Revelation becomes archaic and unsuitable. A written book cannot change, and many things in the Bibles of Religion come to be out of date, inappropriate to new circumstances, and even shocking to an age in which conscience has become more enlightened than it was of old.

The fact that in the same Revelation as that in which palpably immoral commands appear, there occur also jewels of fairest radiance, gems of poetry, pearls of truth, helps us not at all. If moral teachings worthy only of savages occur in Scriptures containing also rare and precious precepts of purest sweetness, the juxtaposition of light and darkness only produces moral chaos. We cannot here appeal to reason or judgment for both must be silent before authority; both rest on the same ground. "Thus saith the Lord" precludes all argument.

Let us take two widely accepted Scriptures, both regarded as authoritative by the respective religions which accept them as coming from a Divine Preceptor or through a human but illuminated being, Moses in the one case, Manu in the other. I am, of course, well aware that in both cases we have to do with books which may contain traditions of their great authors, even sentences transmitted down the centuries. The unravelling of the tangled threads woven into such books is a work needing the highest scholarship and an infinite patience; few of us are equipped for such labour. But let us ignore the work of the Higher Criticism, and take the books as they stand, and the objection raised to them as a basis for morality will at once appear.

Thus we read in the same book: "Thou shalt not avenge, nor bear any grudge against the children of thy people, but thou shalt love thy neighbour as thyself." "The stranger that dwelleth with you shall be unto you as one born among you, and thou shalt love him as thyself, for ye were strangers in the land of Egypt." "Sanctify yourselves therefore and be ye holy." Scores of noble passages, inculcating high morality, might be quoted. But we have also: "If thy brother, the son of thy mother, or thy son, or thy daughter, or the wife of thy bosom, or thy friend which is as thine own soul, entice thee secretly saying, let us go and serve other Gods ... thou shalt not consent unto him nor hearken unto him; neither shalt thine eye pity him, neither shalt thou spare, neither shalt thou conceal him, but thou shalt surely kill him; thine hand shall be first upon him to put him to death." "Thou shalt not suffer a witch to live." A man is told, that he may seize a fair woman in war, and "be her husband and she shall be thy wife. And it shall be that if thou hast no delight in her, then thou shalt let her go whither she will." These teachings and many others like them have drenched Europe with blood and scorched it with fire. Men have grown out of them; they no longer heed nor obey them, for man's reason performs its eclectic work on Revelation, chooses the good, rejects the evil. This is very good, but it destroys Revelation as a basis. Christians have outgrown the lower part of their Revelation, and do not realise that in striving to explain it away they put the axe to the root of its authority.

So also is it with the Institutes of Manu, to take but one example from the great sacred literature of India. There are precepts of the noblest order, and the essence and relative nature of morality is philosophically set out; "the sacred law is thus grounded on the rule of conduct," and He declares that good conduct is the root of

68

further growth in spirituality. Apart from questions of general morality, to which we shall need to refer hereafter, let us take the varying views of women as laid down in the present Smṛti as accepted. On many points there is no wiser guide than parts of this Smṛti, as will be seen in Chapter IV. With regard to the marriage law, Manu says: "Let mutual fidelity continue unto death." Of a father He declares: "No father who knows must take even the smallest gratuity for his daughter; for a man, who through avarice takes a gratuity, is a seller of his offspring." Of the home, He says: "Women must be honoured and adorned by their fathers, husbands, brothers and brothers-in-law who desire happiness. Where women are honoured, there the Devas are pleased; but where they are not honoured, any sacred rite is fruitless." "In that family where the husband is pleased with his wife and the wife with her husband [note the equality], happiness will assuredly be lasting." Food is to be given first in a house to "newly-married women, to infants, to the sick, and to pregnant women". Yet the same Manu is supposed to have taken the lowest and coarsest view of women: "It is the nature of women to seduce men; for that reason the wise are never unguarded with females ... One should not sit in a lonely place with one's mother, sister or daughter; for the senses are powerful, and master even a learned man." A woman must never act "independently, even in her own house," she must be subject to father, husband or (on her husband's death) sons. Women have allotted to them as qualities, "impure desires, wrath, dishonesty, malice and bad conduct". The Shūdra servant is to be "regarded as a younger son"; a slave is to be looked on "as one's shadow," and if a man is offended by him he "must bear it without resentment"; yet the most ghastly punishments are ordered to be inflicted on Shūdras for intruding on certain sacred rites.

The net result is that ancient Revelations, being given for a certain age and certain social conditions, often cannot and ought not to be carried out in the present state of Society; that ancient documents are difficult to verify—often impossible—as coming from those whose names they bear; that there is no guarantee against forgeries, interpolations, glosses, becoming part of the text, with a score of other imperfections; that they contain contradictions, and often absurdities, to say nothing of immoralities. Ultimately every Revelation must be brought to the bar of reason, and as a matter of fact, is so brought in practice, even the most "orthodox" Brāhmaṇa in Hindūism, disregarding all the Shāstraic injunctions which he finds to be impracticable or even inconvenient, while he uses those which suit him to condemn his "unorthodox" neighbours.

No Revelation is accepted as fully binding in any ancient religion, but by common consent the inconvenient parts are quietly dropped, and the evil parts repudiated. Revelation as a basis for morality is impossible. But all sacred books contain much that is pure, lofty, inspiring, belonging to the highest morality, the true utterances of the Sages and Saints of mankind. These precepts will be regarded with reverence by the wise, and should be used as authoritative teaching for the young and the uninstructed as moral textbooks, like—textbooks in other sciences—and as containing moral truths, some of which can be verified by all morally advanced persons, and others verifiable only by those who reach the level of the original teachers.

II

INTUITION

When scholarship, reason and conscience have made impossible the acceptance of Revelation as the bedrock of morality, the student—especially in the West—is apt next to test "Intuition" as a probable basis for ethics. In the East, this idea has not appealed to the thinker in the sense in which the word Intuition is used in the West. The moralist in the East has based ethics on Revelation, or on Evolution, or on Illumination—the last being the basis of the Mystic. Intuition—which by moralists like Theodore Parker, Frances Power Cobb, and many Theists, is spoken of as the "Voice of God" in the human soul—is identified by these with "conscience," so that to base morality on Intuition is equivalent to basing it on conscience, and making the dictate of conscience the categorical imperative, the inner voice which declares authoritatively "Thou shalt," or "Thou shalt not".

Now it is true that for each individual there is no better, no safer, guide than his own conscience and that when the moralist says to the inquirer: "Obey your conscience" he is giving him sound ethical advice. None the less is the thinker faced with an apparently insuperable difficulty in the way of accepting conscience as an ethical basis; for he finds the voice of conscience varying with civilisation, education, race, religion, traditions, customs, and if it be, indeed, the voice of God in man, he cannot but see—in a sense quite different from that intended by the writer—that God "in divers manners spoke in past times". Moreover he observes, as an historical fact, that some of the worst crimes which have disgraced humanity have been done in obedience to the voice of conscience. It is quite clear that Cromwell at Drogheda was obeying conscience, was doing that which he conscientiously believed to be the Will of God; and there is no reason to doubt that a man like Torquemada was also carrying out what he conscientiously believed to be the Divine Will in the war which he waged against heresy through the Inquisition.

In this moral chaos, with such a clash of discordant "Divine Voices," where shall sure guidance be found? One recalls the bitter gibe of Laud to the Puritan, who urged that he must follow his conscience: "Yea, verily; but take heed that thy conscience be not the conscience of a fool."

Conscience speaks with authority, whenever it speaks at all. Its voice is imperial, strong and clear. None the less is it often uninformed, mistaken, in its dictate. There is an Intuition which is verily the voice of the Spirit in man, in the God-illuminated man, which is dealt with in the fifth chapter. But the Intuition recognised in the West, and identified with conscience, is something far other.

For the sake of clarity, we must define what conscience is since we have said what it is not: that it is not the voice of the Spirit in man, that it is not the voice of God.

Conscience is the result of the accumulated experience gained by each man in his previous lives. Each of us is an Immortal Spirit, a Divine fragment, a Self: "A fragment of mine own Self, transformed in the world of life into an immortal Spirit, draweth round itself the senses, of which the mind is the sixth, veiled in Matter." Such is each man. He evolves into manifested powers all the potentialities unfolded in him by virtue of his divine parentage, and this is effected by repeated births into this world, wherein he gathers experience, repeated deaths out of this world into the other twain— the wheel of births and deaths turns in the Triloka, the three worlds—wherein he reaps in pain the results of experiences gathered by disregard of law, and assimilates, transforming into faculty, moral and mental, the results of experience gathered in harmony with law. Having transmuted experience into faculty, he returns to earth for the gathering of new experience, dealt with as before after physical death. Thus the Spirit unfolds, or the man evolves—whichever expression is preferred to indicate this growth. Very similarly doth the physical body grow; a man eats food; digests it, assimilates it, transmutes it into the materials of his body; ill food causes pain, even disease; good food strengthens, and makes for growth. The outer is a reflection of the inner.

Now conscience is the sum total of the experiences in past lives which have borne sweet and bitter fruit, according as they were in accord or disaccord with surrounding natural law. This sum total of physical experiences, which result in increased or diminished life, we call instinct, and it is life-preserving. The sum total of our interwoven mental and moral experiences, in our relations with others, is moral instinct, or conscience, and it is harmonising, impels to "good"—a word which we shall define in our fourth chapter.

Hence conscience depends on the experiences through which we have passed in previous lives, and is necessarily an individual possession. It differs where the past experience is different, as in the savage and the civilised man, the dolt and the talented, the fool and the genius, the criminal and the saint. The voice of God would speak alike in all; the experience of the past speaks differently in each. Hence also the consciences of men at a similar evolutionary level speak alike on broad questions of right and wrong, good and evil. On these the "voice" is clear. But there are many questions whereon past experience fails us, and then conscience fails to speak. We are in doubt; two apparent duties conflict; two ways seem equally right or equally wrong. "I do not know what I ought to do," says the perplexed moralist, hearing no inner voice. In such cases, we must seek to form the best judgment we can, and then act boldly. If unknowingly we disregard some hidden law we shall suffer, and that experience will be added to our sum total, and in similar circumstances in the future, conscience, through the aid of this added experience, will have found a voice.

Hence we may ever, having judged as best we can, act boldly, and learn increased wisdom from the result.

Much moral cowardice, paralysing action, has resulted from the Christian idea of "sin," as something that incurs the "wrath of God," and that needs to be "forgiven," in order to escape an artificial—not a natural—penalty. We gain knowledge by experience, and disregard of a law, where it is not known, should cause us no distress, no remorse, no "repentance," only a quiet mental note that we must in future remember the law which we disregarded and make our conduct harmonise therewith. Where conscience does not speak, how shall we act? The way is well known to all thoughtful people: we first try to eliminate all personal desire from the consideration of the subject on which decision is needed, so that the mental atmosphere may not be rendered a distorting medium by the mists of personal pleasure or pain; next, we place before us all the circumstances, giving each its due weight; then, we decide; the next step depends on whether we believe in Higher Powers or not; if we do, we sit down quietly and alone; we place our decision before us; we suspend all thought, but remain mentally alert—all mental ear, as it were; we ask for help from God, from our Teacher, from our own Higher Self; into that silence comes the decision. We obey it, without further consideration, and then we watch the result, and judge by that of the value of the decision, for it may have come from the higher or from the lower Self. But, as we did our very best, we feel no trouble, even if the decision should be wrong and bring us pain. We have gained an experience, and will do better next time. The trouble, the pain, we have brought on ourselves by our ignorance, we note, as showing that we have disregarded a law, and we profit by the additional knowledge in the future.

Thus understanding conscience, we shall not take it as a basis of morality, but as our best available individual light. We shall judge our conscience, educate it, evolve it by mental effort, by careful observation. As we learn more, our conscience will develop; as we act up to the highest we can see, our vision will become ever clearer, and our ear more sensitive. As muscles develop by exercise, so conscience develops by activity, and as we use our lamp it burns the more brightly. But let it ever be remembered that it is a man's own experience that must guide him, and his own conscience that must decide. To overrule the conscience of another is to induce in him moral paralysis, and to seek to dominate the will of another is a crime.

III

UTILITY

To those whose intelligence and conscience had revolted against the crude and immoral maxims mixed up with noble precepts in Revelation; to those who recognised the impossibility of accepting the varying voices of Intuition as a moral guide; to all those the theory that Morality was based on Utility, came as a welcome and rational relief. It promised a scientific certitude to moral precepts; it left the intellect free to inquire and to challenge; it threw man back on grounds which were found in this world alone, and could be tested by reason and experience; it derived no authority from antiquity, no sanction from religion; it stood entirely on its own feet, independently of the many conflicting elements which were found in the religions of the past and present.

The basis for morality, according to Utility, is the greatest happiness of the greatest number; that which conduces to the greatest happiness of the greatest number is Right; that which does not is Wrong.

This general maxim being laid down, it remains for the student to study history, to analyse experience, and by a close and careful investigation into human nature and human relations to elaborate a moral code which would bring about general happiness and well-being. This, so far, has not been done. Utility has been a "hand-to-mouth" moral basis, and certain rough rules of conduct have grown up by experience and the necessities of life, without any definite investigation into, or codifying of, experience. Man's moral basis as a rule is a compound of partially accepted revelations and partially admitted consciences, with a practical application of the principle of "that which works best". The majority are not philosophers, and care little for a logical basis. They are unconscious empirics, and their morality is empirical.

Mr. Charles Bradlaugh, considering that the maxim did not sufficiently guard the interests of the minority, and that, so far as was possible, these also should be considered and guarded, added another phrase; his basis ran: "The greatest happiness of the greatest number, with the least injury to any." The rule was certainly improved by the addition, but it did not remove many of the objections raised.

It was urged by the Utilitarian that morality had developed out of the social side of human beings; that men, as social animals, desired to live in permanent relations with each other, and that this resulted in the formation of families; men could not be happy in solitude; the persistence of these groups, amid the conflicting interests of the individuals who composed them, could only be secured by recognising that the interests of the majority must prevail, and form the rule of conduct for the whole family. Morality, it was pointed out, thus began in family relations, and conduct which disrupted the family was wrong, while that which strengthened and consolidated it was right. Thus family morality was established. As families congregated together for mutual protection and support, their separate interests as families were found to be conflicting, and so a modus vivendi was sought in the same principle which governed relations within the family: the common interests of the grouped families, the tribe, must prevail over the separate and conflicting interests of the separate families; that which disrupted the tribe was wrong, while that which strengthened and consolidated it was right. Thus tribal morality was established. The next step was taken as tribes grouped themselves together and became a nation, and morality extended so as to include all who were within the nation; that which disrupted the nation was wrong, and that which consolidated and strengthened it was right. Thus national morality was established. Further than that, utilitarian morality has not progressed, and international relations have not yet been moralised; they remain in the savage state, and recognise no moral law. Germany has boldly accepted this position, and declares formally that, for the State, Might is Right, and that all which the State can do for its own aggrandisement, for the increase of its power, it may and ought to do, for there is no rule of conduct to which it owes obedience; it is a law unto itself. Other nations have not formularised the statement in their literature as Germany has done, but the strong nations have acted upon it in their dealings with the weaker nations, although the dawning sense of an international morality in the better of them has led to the defence of international wrong by "the tyrant's plea, necessity". The most flagrant instance of the utter disregard of right and wrong as between nations, is, perhaps, the action of the allied European nations against China—in which the Hun theory of "frightfulness" was enunciated by the German Kaiser—but the history of nations so far is a history of continual tramplings on the weak by the strong, and with the coming to the front of the Christian white nations, and their growth in scientific knowledge and thereby in power, the coloured nations and tribes, whether civilised or savage, have been continually exploited and oppressed. International morality, at present, does not exist. Murder within the family, the tribe, and the nation is marked as a crime, save that judicial murder, capital punishment, is permitted—on the principle of (supposed) Utility. But multiple murder outside the nation—War—is not regarded as criminal, nor is theft "wrong," when committed by a strong nation on a weak one. It may be that out of the widespread misery caused by the present War, some international morality may be developed.

We may admit that, as a matter of historical and present fact, Utility has been everywhere tacitly accepted as the basis of morality, defective as it is as a theory. Utility is used as the test of Revelation, as the test of Intuition, and precepts of Manu, Zarathushtra, Moses, Christ, Muhammad, are acted on, or disregarded, according as they are considered to be useful, or harmful, or impracticable, to be suitable or unsuitable to the times. Inconsistencies in these matters do not trouble the "practical" ordinary man.

The chief attack on the theory of Utility as a basis for morality has come from Christians, and has been effected by challenging the word "happiness" as the equivalent of "pleasure," the "greatest number" as equivalent to "individual," and then denouncing the maxim as "a morality for swine". "Virtue" is placed in antagonism to happiness, and virtue, not happiness, is said to be the right aim for man. This really begs the question, for what is "virtue"? The crux of the whole matter lies there. Is "virtue" opposed to "happiness," or is it a means to happiness? Why is the word "pleasure" substituted for "happiness" when utility is attacked? We may take the second question first.

"Pleasure," in ordinary parlance, means an immediate and transitory form of happiness and usually a happiness of the body rather than of the emotions and the mind. Hence the "swine". A sensual enjoyment is a "pleasure"; union with God would not be called a pleasure, but happiness. An old definition of man's true object is: "To know God, and to enjoy Him for ever." There happiness is clearly made the true end of man. The assailant changes the "greatest happiness of the greatest number" into the "pleasure of the individual," and having created this man of straw, he triumphantly knocks it down.

Does not virtue lead to happiness? Is it not a condition of happiness? How does the Christian define virtue? It is obedience to the Will of God. But he only obeys that Will as "revealed" so far as it agrees with Utility. He no longer slays the heretic, and he suffers the witch to live. He does not give his cloak to the thief who has stolen his coat, but he hands over the thief to the policeman. Moreover, as Herbert Spencer pointed out, he follows virtue as leading to heaven; if right conduct led him to everlasting torture, would he still pursue it? Or would he revise his idea of right conduct? The martyr dies for the truth he sees, because it is easier to him to die than to betray truth. He could not live on happily as a conscious liar. The nobility of a man's character is tested by the things which give him pleasure. The joy in following truth, in striving after the noblest he can see—that is the greatest happiness; to sacrifice present enjoyment for the service of others is not self-denial, but self-expression, to the Spirit who is man.

Where Utility fails is that it does not inspire, save where the spiritual life is already seen to be the highest happiness of the individual, because it conduces to the good of all, not only of the "greatest number". Men who thus feel have inspiration from within themselves and need no outside moral code, no compelling external law. Ordinary men, the huge majority at the present stage of evolution, need either compulsion or inspiration, otherwise they will not control their animal nature, they will not sacrifice an immediate pleasure to a permanent increase of happiness, they will not sacrifice personal gain to the common good. The least developed of these are almost entirely influenced by fear of personal pain and wish for personal pleasure; they will not put their hand into the fire, because they know that fire burns, and no one accuses them of a "low motive" because they do not burn themselves; religion shows them that the results of the disregard of moral and mental law work out in suffering after death as well as before it, and that the results of obedience to such laws similarly work out in post-mortem pleasure. It thus supplies a useful element in the early stages of moral development.

At a higher stage, love of God and the wish to "please Him" by leading an exemplary life is a motive offered by religion, and this inspires to purity and to self-sacrifice; again, this is no more ignoble than the wish to please the father, the mother, the friend. Many a lad keeps pure to please his mother, because he loves her. So religious men try to live nobly to please God, because they love Him. At a higher stage yet, the good of the people, the good of the race, of humanity in the future, acts as a potent inspiration. But this does not touch the selfish lower types. Hence Utility fails as a compelling power with the majority, and is insufficient as motive. Add to this the radical fault that it does not place morality on a universal basis, the happiness of all, that it disregards the happiness of the minority, and its unsatisfactory nature is seen. It has much of truth in it; it enters as a determining factor into all systems of ethics, even where nominally ignored or directly rejected; it is a better basis in theory, though a worse one in practice, than either Revelation or Intuition, but it is incomplete. We must seek further for a solid basis of morality.

IV

EVOLUTION

We come now to the sure basis of morality, the bedrock of Nature, whereon Morality may be built beyond all shaking and change, built as a Science with recognised laws, and in a form intelligible and capable of indefinite expansion. Evolution is recognised as the method of Nature, her method in all her realms, and according to the ascertained laws of Nature, so far as they are known, all wise and thoughtful people endeavour to guide themselves. In making Morality a Science, we give it a binding force, and render it of universal application; moreover, we incorporate into it all the fragments of truth which exist in other systems, and which have lent to them their authority, their appeal to the intellect and the heart.

Let us first define Morality. It is the science of human relations, the Science of Conduct, and its laws, as inviolable, as sure, as changeless, as all other laws of Nature, can be discovered and formulated. Harmony with these laws, like harmony with all other natural laws, is the condition of happiness, for in a realm of law none can move without pain while disregarding law. A law of Nature is the statement of an inviolable and constant sequence external to ourselves and unchangeable by our will, and amid the conditions of these inviolable sequences we live, from these we cannot escape. One choice alone is ours: to live in harmony with them or to disregard them; violate them we cannot, but we can dash ourselves against them; then the law asserts itself in the suffering that results from our flinging ourselves against it, or from our disregarding its existence; its existence is proved as well by the pain that results from our disregard of it, as by the pleasure that results from our harmony with it. Only a fool deliberately and gratuitously disregards a natural law when he knows of its existence; a man shapes his conduct so as to avoid the pain which results from clashing with it, unless he deliberately disregards the pain in view of a result to be brought about, which he considers to be worth more than the purchase price of pain. The Science of Morality, of Right Conduct, "lays down the conditions of harmonious relations between individuals, and their several environments small or large, families, societies, nations, humanity as a whole. Only by the knowledge and observance of these laws can men be either permanently healthy or permanently happy, can they live in peace and prosperity. Where morality is unknown or disregarded, friction inevitably arises, disharmony and pain result; for Nature is a settled Order in the mental and moral worlds as much as in the physical, and only by knowledge of that Order and by obedience to it can harmony, health and happiness be secured."

The religious man sees in the laws of Nature the manifestation of the Divine Nature, and in obedience to and co-operation with them, he sees obedience to and co-operation with the Will of God. The non-religious man sees them as sequences he cannot alter, on harmony with which his happiness, his comfort, depends. In either case they have a binding force. The man belonging to any exoteric religion will modify by them the precepts of his Scriptures, realising that morality rises as Evolution proceeds. He does thus modify scriptural precepts by practical obedience or disregard, whether he do it by theory or not. But it is better that theory and practice should correspond. The intuitionist will understand that conscience, accumulated experience, has developed by experience within these laws. The utilitarian will see that the happiness of all, not only of the greatest number, must be ensured by a true morality, and will understand why Happiness is the result thereof. Manu indicates the various bases very significantly: "The whole Veda is the source of the Sacred Law [Revelation], next the tradition [Conscience] and the virtuous conduct of those who know [Utility], also the customs of holy men [Evolution] and self-satisfaction [Mysticism]" (ii, 6.). It is true that happiness can result only by harmony with law, harmony with the Divine Will which is embodied in law—we need not quarrel over names—and the Science of Right Conduct, "by establishing righteousness brings about Happiness". It may therefore be truly said that the object of Morality is Universal Happiness. Why the doing of a right action causes a flow of happiness in the doer, even in the midst of a keen temporary pain entailed by it, we shall see under "Mysticism".

The moment we base Morality on Evolution, we see that it must change with the stage of evolution reached, and that the duty—that which ought to be done—of the civilised and highly advanced man is not the same as the duty of the savage. "One set of duties for men in the Kṛta age, different ones in the Tretā and in the Dvāpara, and another the Kali." (Manusmṛti, i, 85.) Different ages bring new duties. But if Morality be based on Evolution we can at once define what is "Right" and what is "Wrong". That is Right which subserves Evolution; that is Wrong which antagonises it. Or in other words, for those of us who believe that God's method for this world is the evolutionary: that is Right which co-operates with His Will; that is wrong which works against it. "Revelation" is an attempt to state this at any given time; "Intuition" is the result of successful attempts to do this; "Utility" is the application of observed results of happiness and misery which flow from obedience to this, or disregard thereof.

Evolution is the unfolding and manifestation of life-energies, the unfolding of the capacities of consciousness, the manifestation of these ever-increasing capacities in ever-improving and more plastic forms. The primary truth of Morality, as of Religion and of Science, is the Unity of Life. One Life ever unfolding in endless varieties of forms; the essence of all beings is the same, the inequalities are the marks of the stage of its unfoldment.

When we base Morality on Evolution, we cannot have, it is obvious, one cut and dry rule for all. Those who want cut and dry rules must go to their Scriptures for them, and even then, as the rules in the Scriptures are contradictory—both as between Scriptures and within any given Scripture—they must call in the help of Intuition and Utility in the making of their code, in their selective process. This selective process will be largely moulded by the public opinion of their country and age, emphasising some precepts and ignoring others, and the code will be the expression of the average morality of the time. If this clumsy and uncertain fashion of finding a rule of conduct does not suit us, we must be willing to exert our intelligence, to take a large view of the evolutionary process, and to deduce our moral precepts at any given stage by applying our

86

reason to the scrutiny of this process at that stage. This scrutiny is a laborious one; but Truth is the prize of effort in the search therefor, it is not an unearned gift to the slothful and the careless.

This large view of the evolutionary process shows us that it is best studied in two great divisions: the first from the savage to the highly civilised man who is still working primarily for himself and his family, still working for private ends predominantly; and the second, at present but sparsely followed, in which the man, realising the supreme claim of the whole upon its part, seeks the public good predominantly, renounces individual advantages and private gains, and consecrates himself to the service of God and of man. The Hindu calls the first section of evolution the Pravṛtti Mārga, the Path of Forthgoing; the second the Nivṛtti Mārga, the Path of Return. In the first, the man evolves by taking; in the second, by giving. In the first, he incurs debts; in the second, he pays them. In the first, he acquires; in the second, he renounces. In the first, he lives for the profit of the smaller self; in the second, for the service of the One Self. In the first, he claims Rights; in the second, he discharges Duties.

Thus Morality is seen from two view-points, and the virtues it comprises fall into two groups. Men are surrounded on every side by objects of desire, and the use of these is to evoke the desire to possess them, to stimulate exertion, to inspire efforts, and thus to make faculty, capacity—strength, intelligence, alertness, judgment, perseverance, patience, fortitude. Those who regard the world as God-emanated and God-guided, must inevitably realise that the relation of man—susceptible to pleasure and pain by contact with his environment—to his environment—filled with pleasure and pain-giving objects—must be intended to provoke in man the desire to possess the pleasure-giving, to avoid the pain-giving. In fact,

God's lures to exertion are pleasures; His warnings are pains and the interplay between man and environment causes evolution. The man who does not believe in God has only to substitute the word "Nature" for "God" and to leave out the idea of design, and the argument remains the same: man's relation to his environment provokes exertion, and thus evolution. A man on the Path of Forthgoing will, at first, seize everything he desires, careless of others, and will gradually learn, from the attacks of the despoiled, some respect for the rights of others; the lesson will be learnt more quickly by the teaching of more advanced men—Rṣhis, Founders of Religions, Sages, and the like—who tell him that if he kills, robs, tramples on others, he will suffer. He does all these things; he suffers; he learns—his post-mortem lives helping him much in the learning. Later on, he lives a more controlled and regulated life, and he may blamelessly enjoy the objects of desire, provided he injure none in the taking. Hindūism lays down, as the proper pursuits for the household life, the gaining of wealth, the performance of the duties of the position held, the gratification of desire. The desires will become subtler and more refined as intelligence fashions them and as emotions replace passions; but throughout the treading of the Path of Forthgoing, the "desire for fruit" is the necessary and blameless motive for exertion. Without this, the man at this stage of evolution becomes lethargic and does not evolve. Desire subserves Evolution, and it is Right. The gratification of Desire may lead a man to do injury to others, and as soon as he has developed enough to understand this, then the gratification becomes wrong, because, forgetting the Unity, he has inflicted harm on one who shares life with him, and has thus hampered evolution. The sense of Unity is the root-Love, the Uniter, and Love is the expression of the attraction of the separated towards union; out of Love, controlled by reason and by the desire for the happiness of all, grow all

Virtues, which are but permanent, universal, specialised forms of love. So also is the sense of Separateness the root-Hate, the Divider, the expression of the repulsion of the separated from each other. Out of this grow all Vices, the permanent, universal, specialised forms of Hate. That which Love does for the Beloved, that Virtue does for all who need its aid, so far as its power extends. That which Hate wreaks on the Abhorred, that Vice does to all who obstruct its path, so far as its power extends.

"Virtues and Vices are fixed emotional states. The Virtues are fixed Love-emotions, regulated and controlled by enlightened intelligence seeing the Unity; the Vices are fixed Hate-emotions, strengthened and intensified by the unenlightened intelligence, seeing the separateness." (Universal Text Book, ii, 32.) It is obvious that virtues are constructive and vices destructive, for Love holds together, while Hate disintegrates. Yet the modified form of Hate— antagonism, competition—had its part to play in the earlier stages of human evolution, developing strength, courage, and endurance, and while Love built up Nations within themselves, Hate made each strong against its competitor. And within Nations, there has been conflict of classes, class and caste war, and all this modified and softened by a growing sense of a common good, until Competition, the characteristic of the Path of Forthgoing tends to change into Co-operation, the characteristic of the Path of Return. The Path of Forthgoing must still be trodden by many, but the number is decreasing; more and more are turning towards the Path of Return. Ideals are formulated by the leaders of Humanity, and the Ideals held up to-day are increasingly those of Love and of Service. "During the first stage, man grasps at everything he desires and develops a strong individuality by conflict; in the second, he shares all he has, and yokes that individuality to service; ever-increasing separation is the key-note of the one; ever-increasing unity is the key-note of the other. Hence we need not brand as evil the rough aggression and the fierce struggles of barbarous times; they were a necessary stage of growth and were at that stage Right, and in the divine plan. But now those days are over, strength has been won; the time has come when the separated selves must gradually draw together, and to co-operate with the divine Will which is working for union is the Right. The Right which is the outcome of Love, directed by reason, at the present stage of evolution, then, seeks an ever-increasing realisation of Unity, a drawing together of the separated selves. That which by establishing harmonious relations makes for Unity is Right; that which divides and disintegrates, which makes for separation, is Wrong." (ibid., 10, 11.)

Hindūism, on which the whole of this is based, has added to this broad criterion the division of a life into four stages, to each of which appropriate virtues are assigned: the Student Period, with its virtues of perfect continence, industry, frugality, exertion; the Household Period, with its virtue of duties appropriate to the position, the earning and enjoying of wealth, the gratification of desires; the Retirement Period, with the virtues of the renouncing of worldly gain and of sacrifice; the Ascetic Period, of complete renunciation, meditation and preparation for post-mortem life. These indications make more easy the decisions as to Right and Wrong.

The more we think upon and work out into detail this view of Morality as based on Evolution, the more we realise its soundness, and the more we find that the moral law is as discoverable by observation, by reason, and by experiment, as any other law of Nature. If a man disregards it, either ignorantly or wilfully, he suffers. A man may disregard physical hygienic and sanitary laws because of his ignorance; none the less will he suffer from physical disease. A man may disregard moral laws because of ignorance; none the less will he suffer from moral disease. The sign of disease in both cases is pain and unhappiness; experts in both cases warn us, and if we disregard the warning, we learn its truth later by experience. There is no hurry; but the law is sure. Working with the law, man evolves swiftly with happiness; working against it, he evolves slowly with pain. In either case, he evolves, advancing joyously as a free man, or scourged onwards as a slave. The most obstinate fool in life's class, refusing to learn, fortunately dies and cannot quite escape after death the knowledge of his folly.

Let the reader try for himself the solution of moral problems, accepting, as a hypothesis, the facts of evolution and of the two halves of its huge spiral, and see for himself if this view does not offer a rational, intelligible, practical meaning to the much-vexed words, Right and Wrong. Let him see how it embraces all that is true in the other bases suggested, is their summation, and rationalises their precepts. He will find that Morality is no longer dependent on the maxims of great Teachers—though indeed they proclaimed its changeless laws—nor on the imperfect resultant of individual experiences, nor on the happiness of some only of the great human family, but that it inheres in the very nature of things, an essential law of happy life and ordered progress. Then indeed is Morality founded on a basis that cannot be moved; then indeed can it speak with an imperial authority the "ought" that must be obeyed; then it unfolds its beauty as humanity evolves to its perfecting, and leads to Bliss Eternal, the Brahman Bliss, where the human will, in fullest freedom, accords itself in harmony with the divine.

V

MYSTICISM

Mysticism cannot be spoken of as a basis of morality in the sense in which Revelation, Intuition, Utility and Evolution are bases, for it is valid only for the individual, not for everybody, for the true Mystic, the dictates of the Outer or Inner God are imperial, compelling, but to any one else they are entirely unauthoritative. None the less, as the influence of the Mystic is wide-reaching, and his dicta are accepted by many as a trustworthy revelation—are not all revelations communicated by Mystics?—or as the intuition of an illuminated conscience, or as showing the highest utility, or as the result of an evolution higher than the normal, it is worth while to consider their value.

Mysticism is the realisation of God, of the Universal Self. It is attained either as a realisation of God outside the Mystic, or within himself. In the first case, it is usually reached from within a religion, by exceptionally intense love and devotion, accompanied by purity of life, for only "the pure in heart shall see God". The external means are prayer to and meditation on the Object of devotion—Shrī Rāma, Shrī Kṛṣhṇa, the Lord Jesus—long continued and persevering, and the devotee realises his Divinity by ecstacy attaining Union thereby. Such Mystics are, for the most part, valuable to the world as creating an atmosphere of spirituality, which raises the general level of religious feeling in those who come within its area; India has especially profited by the considerable number of such Mystics found within its borders in past times, and to a lesser extent to-day; every one who practises, for instance, meditation, knows that it is easier here than elsewhere, and all sensitive persons feel the Indian "atmosphere". Outside this, such Mystics occasionally write valuable books, containing high ideals of the spiritual life. As a rule, they do not concern themselves with the affairs of the outer world, which they regard as unimportant. Their cry continually is that the world is evil, and they call on men to leave it, not to improve it. To them God and the world are in opposition, "the world, the flesh, and the devil" are the three great enemies of the spiritual life. In the West, this is almost universal, for in the Roman Catholic Church seclusion is the mark of the religious life, and "the religious" are the monk and the nun, the "religious" and the "secular" being in opposition. In truth, where the realisation of God outside himself is sought by the devotee, seclusion is a necessity for success, if only for the time which is required for meditation, the essential preliminary of ecstacy. In the very rare Mystics of non-Catholic communions, full ecstacy is scarcely, if at all, known or even recognised; an overpowering sense of the divine Presence is experienced, but it is a Presence outside the worshipper; it is accompanied with a deliberate surrender of the will to God, and a feeling on the part of the man that he becomes an instrument of the divine Will; this he carries with him into outer life, and, undirected by love and the illuminated reason, it often lands the half-developed Mystic into fanaticism and cruelty; no one who has read Oliver Cromwell's letters can deny that he was a Mystic, half-developed, and it is on him that Lord Rosebery founded his dictum of the formidable nature of the "practical Mystic"; the ever present sense of a divine Power behind himself gives such a man a power that ordinary men cannot successfully oppose; but this sense affords no moral basis, as, witness the massacre of Drogheda. Such a Mystic, belonging to a particular religion, as he always does, takes the revelation of his religion as his moral code, and Cromwell felt himself as the avenging sword of his God, as did the Hebrews fighting with the Amalekites. No man who accepts a revelation as his guide can be regarded as more than partially a Mystic. He has the Mystic temperament only, and that undoubtedly gives him a strength far beyond the strength of those who have it not.

The true Mystic, realising God, has no need of any Scriptures, for he has touched the source whence all Scriptures flow. An "enlightened" Brāhmaṇa, says Shrī Kṛṣhṇa, has no more need of the Vedas, than a man needs a tank in a place which is overflowing with water. The value of cisterns, of reservoirs, is past, when a man is seated beside an ever-flowing spring. As Dean Inge has pointed out, Mysticism is the most scientific form of religion, for it bases itself, as does all science, on experience and experiment— experiment being only a specialised form of experience, devised either to discover or to verify.

We have seen the Mystic who realises God outside himself and seeks Union with Him. There remains the most interesting, the most effective form of Mysticism, the realisation by a man of God within himself. Here meditation is also a necessity, and the man who is born with a high capacity for concentration is merely a man who has practised it in previous lives. A life or lives of study and seclusion often precede a life of tremendous and sustained activity in the physical world. The realisation is preceded by control of the body, control of the emotions and control of the mind, for the power to hold these in complete stillness is necessary, if a man is to penetrate into those depths of his own nature in which alone is to be found the shrine of the inner God. The subtle music of that sphere is drowned by the clatter of the lower bodies as the most exquisite notes of the Vīṇā are lost in the crude harsh sound of the harmonium. The Voice of the Silence can only be heard in the silence, and all the desires of the heart must be paralysed ere can arise in the tranquillity of senses and mind, the glorious majesty of the Self. Only in the desert of loneliness rises that Sun in all His glory, for all objects that might cloud His dawning must vanish; only "when half-Gods go," does God arise. Even the outer God must hide, ere the Inner God can manifest; the cry of agony of the Crucified must be wrung from the tortured lips; "My God, my God, why hast Thou forsaken me?" precedes the realisation of the God within.

Through this all Mystics pass who are needed for great service in the world, those whom Mr. Bagshot so acutely calls "materialised Mystics". The Mystics who find God outside themselves are the "unmaterialised" Mystics, and they serve the world in the ways above mentioned; but the other, as Mr. Bagshot points out, transmute their mystic thought into "practical energy," and these become the most formidable powers known in the physical world. All that is based on injustice, fraud and wrong may well tremble when one of these arises, for the Hidden God has become manifest, and who may bar His way?

Such Mystics wear none of the outer signs of the "religious"—their renunciation is within, not without, there is no parade of outer holiness, no outer separation from the world; Janaka the King, Kṛṣṇa the Warrior-Statesman, are of these; clothed in cotton cloth or cloth of gold, it matters not; poor or rich, it boots not; failing or succeeding, it is naught, for each apparent failure is the road to fuller success, and both are their servants, not their masters; victory ever attends them, to-day or a century hence is equal, for they live in Eternity, and with them it is ever To-day. Possessing nothing, all is theirs; holding everything, nothing belongs to them. Misconception, misrepresentation, they meet with a smile, half-amused, all-forgiving; the frowns, the taunts, the slanders of the men they live to serve are only the proofs of how much these foolish ones need their help, and how should these foolish ones hurt those on whom the Peace of the Eternal abides?

These Mystics are a law unto themselves, for the inner law has replaced the external compulsion. More rigid, for it is the law of their own nature; more compelling, for it is the Voice of the divine Will; more exacting, for no pity, no pardon, is known to it; more all-embracing, for it sees the part only in the whole.

But it has, it ought to have, no authority outside the Mystic himself. It may persuade, it may win, it may inspire, but it may not claim obedience as of right. For the Voice of the God within only becomes authoritative for another when the God within that other self answers the Mystic's appeal, and he recognises an ideal that he could not have formulated, unaided, for himself. The Mystic may shine as a Light, but a man must see with his own eyes, and there lies the world's safety; the materialised Mystic, strong as he is, cannot, by virtue of the God within him, enslave his fellow-men.

9 781618 959973